TEACHING YOUR CHILD

THE LANGUAGE OF

SOCIAL SUCCESS

Teaching Your Child
the Language of
Social Success

Marshall P. Duke, Ph.D.
Stephen Nowicki, Jr., Ph.D
Elisabeth A. Martin, M.Ed.

illustrations by Vicky Holifield

PEACHTREE
ATLANTA

ACKNOWLEDGMENTS

For the research on which this book is based, we are indebted to the members of the Emory Dyssemia Group at Emory University as well as to the undergraduate researchers who worked with us in Great Britain over the past decade. Their commitment and energies have been invigorating to us and have served as the impetus for many of the things we have already learned and will learn in the future.

Special thanks go also to the amazing professionals at Peachtree Publishers, who not only wanted to produce a sound book which would make a difference in children's lives but also make its authors feel very much valued and special. Thanks to Margaret Quinlin, Kathy Landwehr, Stephanie Thomas, and for her wonderful illustrations, Vicky Holifield. Thanks also to the talented Laura Seeley, whose beautiful cover captures the essence of this book.

We thank the teachers who have taught us through applying our concepts in their work with children. We thank the children who looked at photos, listened to audiotapes, and walked up to "stimuli" and stopped at comfortable distances. They helped us to learn about the nature of nonverbal language development. We thank our own children and grandchildren for being the laboratory that lives before our eyes.

Finally and inexorably, we continue to thank our spouses, Sara, Kaaren, and David. Their support has never wavered in form or intensity from the beginning. We are sure in our hearts that it will always be as it has always been.

MPD, SN, ECM
Atlanta, Georgia and Newcastle, England 1996

℗

Published by
PEACHTREE PUBLISHERS, LTD.
494 Armour Circle NE, Atlanta, Georgia 30324

Text © 1996 Marshall P. Duke, Stephen Nowicki, Jr., Elisabeth Martin
Interior illustrations © 1996 Vicky Holifield

Cover illustration by Laura L. Seeley
Cover design by Loraine M. Balcsik
Book design by Terri Fox

Manufactured in the United States of America

10 9 8 7 6 5 4 3 2

Library of Congress Cataloging-in-Publication Data

Duke, Marshall P.
    Teaching your child the language of social success / Marshall P. Duke, Stephen Nowicki, Jr., Elisabeth A. Martin.
        p. cm.
    Includes bibliographical references.
    ISBN 1-56145-126-6
    1. Nonverbal communication in children. 2. Interpersonal communication in children. 3. Social interaction in children. I. Nowicki, Stephen. II. Martin, Elisabeth A. III. Title.
BF723.C57D85 1996
155.4′ 1369—dc20   96-4762
                                                                                                    CIP

TABLE OF CONTENTS

How to Use This Book

Everyone knows children who just seem to get life "right." They are the ones for whom all the lights are green, the ones always invited to parties, always sought after as friends. Their social behavior seems almost effortless as they glide through their daily interactions. Try as they may to be fair, teachers often find such children the most pleasant of all their students and favor them without even realizing it. Research is now showing that these youngsters continue to succeed not only throughout their schooling, but also throughout the rest of their lives.

The British psychologist, Rom Harré, once said that people are like places and, like places, there are some that are so pleasant to visit that you stay long and come back often. Likewise, there are some places that you do not enjoy visiting, that you leave as soon as you can, and that you rarely return to, unless you must. During more than twenty years of research dealing with the qualities that make people "nice places to visit," we have focused on children who have difficulty establishing and maintaining social relationships, as well as on those for whom the lights are always green.

In our first book, *Helping the Child Who Doesn't Fit In*, we addressed the problems of children with identifiable disorders in nonverbal language usage. About 10 percent of children suffer from deficiencies so severe that they experience social rejection. Another 10 percent demonstrate such an unusually high proficiency in nonverbal skills that they almost always excel in social interactions. *Teaching Your Child the Language of Social Success* addresses the vast majority of children in between these two extremes, children who have developed a degree of skill in nonverbal communication, but who need improvement in some areas of this "second language." In this book, we reintroduce the fundamentals of nonverbal communication and build on that foundation to broaden the applicability of our research. We now turn our attention to achieving social success.

Decades of research and clinical observation have led us to believe that we have found a major source of success in children's interpersonal relationships as well as in those of adults. The ability to utilize nonverbal language effectively is the very basis of solid and satisfying social and vocational success throughout life; the absence of this ability is an identifiable and correctable cause of social difficulties.

When we say "nonverbal communication," you may be thinking we mean "body language," and you may be wondering why some children are good at this and others aren't. Well, "body language" is really only a part of nonverbal communication. Indeed, many believe that nonverbal communication is a fully developed language that functions side by side with verbal language. The reason why some children don't learn this nonverbal language, or why many children do not develop it as fully as they could, is that we as parents and teachers rarely teach it formally. While children go to school to learn the grammar of the spoken language, they receive little formal training in the skills of nonverbal language. These skills are typically taught informally (often without full awareness of their importance) by parents and family members, and they are often learned through observation. Since children primarily learn nonverbal language informally, in a hit-or-miss way, many do not learn as much as they need to—or could—about one or more of the nonverbal rules. Thus, they may not have a thoroughly developed set of the skills that are so basic to social success. They arrive at school armed with their parentally taught and practiced knowledge of the proverbial three "R's"—reading, 'riting and 'rithmetic—but they may be ill-prepared for the fourth "R"—*relationships*. It is our belief that parents and teachers can help with this fourth "R," that they can help children to learn the language of interpersonal relationships, and that they can thereby improve their chances for social success and the benefits that derive from it.

In this book, we have attempted to help parents and teachers address this situation in three major ways:

1. by providing information that will allow them to identify forms of nonverbal language;
2. by describing ways in which they can systematically and informally evaluate children's abilities in nonverbal language usage; and
3. by giving them exercises which can help children develop their fullest potential in nonverbal language and maximize their chances for social success.

PART ONE

WHAT IS NONVERBAL COMMUNICATION?

1

THE LANGUAGE OF RELATIONSHIPS

Social success is not always the result of doing certain things. Quite often, it results from *not* doing something, such as not staring at people in an elevator, not touching people in inappropriate places, or not making certain offensive gestures.

A mother and her daughter got on an elevator. The other passengers arranged themselves equidistantly from each other, faced forward, and looked up at the changing numbers. The little girl turned so she was facing the back of the elevator and stared at the passengers, who became very uncomfortable. Her mother told her to turn around and face the door. The little girl asked, "Why?" The mother, who could sense the passengers' anxiety, was hard pressed to come up with a logical answer.

This little girl broke one of the rules of nonverbal communication. The mother knew that her daughter's behavior was inappropriate, but she found it difficult to verbalize the nonverbal etiquette of elevator use.

THE GRAMMAR OF NONVERBAL COMMUNICATION

Although the grammar of nonverbal language is unwritten, there are still rules for its use. Sociologist Thomas Scheff labeled these unwritten rules residual rules. *Residual rules* are the nonverbal rules for any given situation, and they are usually noticed only when they are broken. They are not written down or formalized, yet we must follow them if we are to make the people around us comfortable, and if we want to "fit in." If we know and apply these rules especially well, we do more than fit in—we succeed socially. As Albert Mehrabian once said, "Verbal cues are definable by an explicit dictionary meaning and by rules of syntax, but there are only vague and informal explanations of the significance of various nonverbal behaviors."

Residual rules cover an immense number of behaviors and situations, and all of these must be learned well if we are to be interpersonally effective. It is difficult to be certain about how, where, and from whom we learn these rules for using proper nonverbal communication. Some nonverbal patterns may be part of our behavioral repertoire at birth. For example, blind and deaf children appear to show socially appropriate facial expressions reflecting emotional states, just as their sighted and hearing peers do. These inborn behaviors are important, but most would agree that the great majority of rules are learned in informal ways.

The very informality of the process, compared to the structured lessons of grammar, often makes the learning of nonverbal skills a hit-or-miss affair in which some children have much training and others relatively little. Great gaps in knowledge can result in broad differences in social success, ranging from the child who moves through life with relative grace and ease to the youngster who is rejected by peers "for no apparent reason." Such gaps can occur in one or more of the following six areas:

- **Paralanguage**: All those aspects of sound which communicate emotion and are used either independently or with words fall into this group. Whistling and humming are paralanguage, as are tone, intensity, and loudness of voice.

- **Facial Expressions:** Facial movements and poses communicate emotion. Effective eye contact and the appropriate use of facial expressions like smiling are two of the most frequently noted characteristics of socially adept children.

- **Postures and Gestures:** Hand and arm movements that communicate meaning are called gestures; positions of the entire body that convey meaning are called postures. Both gestures and postures can convey messages that conflict with spoken words, confusing communication efforts.

- **Interpersonal Distance (Space) and Touch:** We all carry a portable territory and boundaries around with us. If a child stands too close to others while having a conversation, that child is violating the rules of personal space. Similarly, a child who touches others inappropriately, either in terms of the location or the intensity of that contact, is breaking one of the unwritten laws of touch and stands an excellent chance of being rejected without knowing why.

- **Rhythm and Time:** Speech patterns, attitudes, and speed of movement or speech all fall into the category of rhythm. A child from New York City has a different "rhythm" than a child from Baton Rouge, Louisiana. Their speech patterns and attitudes are indicative of the differences in their environments. Problems can arise when they are "out of sync" with one another. This area also includes habits of time management, such as arriving promptly or being late for appointments.

- **Objectics:** Personal hygiene and style of dress indicate that individuals are part of a group, and keep them from being singled out as strange or different. People frequently judge others by the clothes they wear, the way those clothes are worn, and their personal hygiene.

THE VOCABULARY OF COMMUNICATION

Language is basically a set of symbols whose meanings are agreed upon by all those who use them. Thus, an English speaker does not need to have an actual object in hand when using the word "apple" in order for others to understand what the word means. (Of course, that same object would be symbolized differently in other languages, such as French (*pomme*), German (*Apfel*), or Spanish (*manzana*).) Just as the word "apple" communicates an idea that is held inside the mind of a person, a smile also symbolizes something that cannot be seen—in this case a feeling of happiness or a state of friendliness. Unlike verbal languages, however, nonverbal "signs," such as smiles and frowns, tend to be more universal.

Nonverbal language is the mother tongue of the human relationship.

Linguists tell us that within a specific language, there are two sublanguages. *Expressive language* uses symbols to "encode" messages—to put them into words or other symbols. *Receptive language* is the ability to "decode" messages—to interpret accurately their intended meanings. Expressive verbal language includes the ability to speak or write using words; receptive verbal language involves the abilities to understand the meaning of those words, whether they are spoken or written.

Expressive nonverbal language is the communication of internal states such as happiness, sadness, or fear, through facial expressions, postures, voice tones, and other methods. Receptive nonverbal language interprets those same signals. It is our belief that nonverbal language has its own vocabulary, just as verbal communication does, but that the two play different roles in our lives. Verbal language is the language of the intellect, of the idea, of the school. Nonverbal language is the mother tongue of the human relationship.

How Nonverbal Communication Works

When verbal and nonverbal language convey conflicting messages, people almost always tend to believe the nonverbal message. Nonverbal language is usually seen by others as a reliable reflection of how we actually feel. A classic set of studies by Albert Mehrabian showed that in face-to-face interactions, 55 percent of the emotional meaning of a message is expressed through facial, postural, and gestural means, and 38 percent of the emotional meaning is transmitted through tone of voice. Only 7 percent of emotional meaning is actually expressed with words.

The ability to "speak" and to "listen" nonverbally—or the ability to communicate expressively and receptively—allows us to interact with one another more effectively. If we can clearly sense the feelings and attitudes of others, we can relate to them in ways that respect and value their feelings and thereby insure that our needs and wishes are clearly expressed in return. We enjoy being with people who understand us and are easy to understand themselves. Serious misunderstandings can occur if we fail to interpret nonverbal messages correctly, or if we send nonverbal messages that do not accurately reflect our emotions.

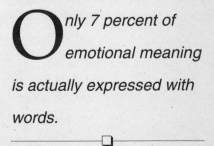

Only 7 percent of emotional meaning is actually expressed with words.

Tom decides to go to a movie—a light comedy. After paying for his ticket, he enters the theater and looks around. There are only five other people in the theater, which is large enough for two hundred. Tom walks down the aisle and stops where one person is sitting in the middle of a row. He walks into that row until he reaches the seat next to the stranger and promptly sits down.

What would you conclude about Tom after observing his behavior? We believe that if you focus on his seat selection, you will conclude that Tom is behaving strangely. Think of yourself as being that one person sitting in the middle of a row in a nearly empty movie theater that can hold hundreds of people. What are your conclusions about Tom, and how does he make you feel? If you are like the participants in our workshops, you think that something is psychologically wrong with Tom, and he makes you anxious, uneasy, uncomfortable, and afraid. Tom's nonverbal language is likely to spur you to action—to get up and leave!

When we see someone else make a mistake in verbal communication, we may make judgments about that person's intellectual abilities. In contrast, when we see a person commit an error in nonverbal communication, as Tom did, we are more prone to think of that person as socially inept and even unlikable. We might sympathetically look upon a person who makes mistakes in verbal communication as poorly educated or ignorant. On the other hand, we are likely to regard a person who makes errors in nonverbal communication as strange or weird. Children often apply cruel names to those who—for reasons they cannot ascertain—do not follow nonverbal social rules. While children's levels of verbal ability undoubtedly have something to do with their social success, it is likely that their social success will be affected even more significantly by their nonverbal language skills.

Put more simply, being intelligent or well educated does not automatically make you socially successful—everyone knows someone who provides supporting evidence for this claim! People without nonverbal language skills often seem unpredictable and confusing. Such people may even threaten our feelings of safety and security. People who do not possess nonverbal language skills unknowingly put up a barrier between themselves and others, whereas people who know and follow the rules of nonverbal language make others feel comfortable—they are "good places to visit."

Another reason that nonverbal communication is so important in our relationships to one another is the fact that, unlike verbal language, which occurs intermittently, nonverbal communication occurs continually. The nonstop nature of nonverbal communication has significant implications for human interaction. Recent surveys indicate that the average person spends less than forty minutes a day in verbal conversation with others. But verbal silence does not mean that nothing is being said; whenever we are around others, we are communicating nonverbally—whether we want to or not. People cannot help being affected by our facial expressions, our posture, or how close we stand to them. Likewise, we cannot avoid being affected by the nonverbal behavior of other people.

Some researchers sum up the nonstop nature of nonverbal communication by saying, "You cannot *not* communicate nonverbally!" Because nonverbal communication is continuous, nonverbal strengths or weaknesses will generally have a greater impact on social interactions than equivalent levels of verbal ability.

- Imagine a boy who mutters, "Let's be friends." He is communicating his desire for friends inefficiently; he sends one verbal signal over the span of only a few seconds, and his signal reaches only a few children within earshot.

- In contrast, think of a girl who always smiles at others while listening intently and making strong eye contact. The entire time she is around people, her expression is communicating her friendliness and attracting others to her. Her signals are much more likely to produce the desired results.

All of us like to be around people who smile at us and who look at us directly and with interest. We cannot help but respond positively. A chain of positive interactions often begins and continues toward exchanged greetings, shared social activities, and eventual friendship. Therefore, those who are adept at nonverbal language stand to gain tremendous benefits, while those who use it poorly seem destined to experience widespread confusion and frustration—without ever knowing the reason why!

Y*ou cannot NOT communicate nonverbally!*

Those fortunate individuals who can make friends easily and maintain satisfactory relationships are usually unaware that the source of their prowess lies in their nonverbal communication. Because the reasons for their effectiveness are out of their awareness, they find it very difficult to explain their skills to others. The methods of teaching nonverbal language skills, therefore, have long remained underdeveloped and have eluded the grasp of most parents and teachers.

Since nonverbal behavior and communication are learned, parents and teachers can help teach children the skills they are lacking. Because nonverbal responses are seen as more reliable indicators of our true feelings than verbal responses, paying attention to and understanding the nonverbal social behaviors of others is an important communication skill to possess (Ekman and Friesen 1971; Mehrabian 1987; Bailey 1995).

When parents, teachers, and support staff are aware of nonverbal communication disorders, they can provide children with appropriate, well-planned activities to avoid or remediate these difficulties.

EXPRESSIVE AND RECEPTIVE LANGUAGE DISORDERS

As with any skill, one can observe strengths and weaknesses in the use of language. While the major thrust of this book is on building strengths, much can be learned about the importance of language forms by examination of what happens when children's skills are noticeably weak.

Children with receptive verbal language deficits have difficulty understanding the information they receive. People with dyslexia, a receptive verbal deficit, have trouble reading the words printed on a page, even though they have average or above-average intelligence. Because they don't receive information accurately, dyslexics mix up letters and words. For example, they may reverse the letter 'd' to read 'b,' so that the word "dog" could be read as "bog."

Some people also suffer from expressive verbal language disorders. Children with problems of this type have trouble expressing or producing verbal information. For example, a child might read the word "may" correctly, but when he or she attempts to write or articulate it, the result is the word "yam."

Verbal language skills and their associated verbal language deficits have nonverbal parallels. In much the same way that dyslexics have difficulty with the written word (*dys* = difficulty, *lexic* = words), many children cannot understand or "read" the quieter messages of others. In our earlier book, *Helping the Child Who Doesn't Fit In*, we coined the term *dyssemia*, meaning a difficulty (*dys*) in using nonverbal signs or signals (*semes*). For example, a person with receptive facial dyssemia may misread a sad face as an angry one, and as a result may respond to downcast eyes with a frown or glare.

While children receive ample education in verbal language skills, little is typically done in school or at home to help them develop their nonverbal language abilities. Nevertheless, most children come to adolescence and adulthood with verbal skills adequate to meet the intellectual and vocational requirements that society places upon them. However, there are large numbers of children—all with the ability to learn and use nonverbal language—who do not develop those skills fully and therefore do not adequately understand how to establish and maintain effective interpersonal relationships. This book can help reduce that gap in children's educations.

Before moving on, we want to alert you to some characteristics often found in children with dyssemia. It is important to realize first that these dyssemic children generally want to participate with others in play or in family activities; they neither choose to be alone nor seek rejection. They want to get along with others and do what is expected of them, although that is not always reflected in their behavior.

Here are some indicators of dyssemia, derived from our research as well as from the work of Doris Johnson, Helmer Myklebust, and other investigators. The dyssemic child often:

- is described by parents and teachers as tactless and insensitive

- is described by other children as dumb, but is usually average or above average in intelligence

- is described by parents as being "different" from others since infancy

- is seen by parents and teachers as lacking in social maturity

- has difficulty perceiving danger

- has difficulty understanding rules and sequences of games

- has difficulty recognizing the contingency between his or her behavior and the consequences of that behavior

- feels some or all of the following feelings: sad, bewildered, lonely, confused, and anxious

- perseveres in action or activity even when it leads to punishment or rejection

- is inconsistent; will be accurate in some aspect of nonverbal communication one day but not the next.

Fortunately, children with dyssemic problems severe enough to evolve into the social-perceptual disability described above are rare. There are far more children who have the skills necessary to produce average to above-average social relationships. But there are other children who are so highly talented in the use of nonverbal language that they fit into a category we call *eusemic*.

Thus, just as there are children who have difficulties in using expressive and receptive nonverbal language, there are also youngsters who are especially good at communicating without words. Our research has indicated, in fact, that just as nonverbal deficits—dyssemias—are associated with social rejection, nonverbal strengths are associated with a high degree of social success. We have created the word *eusemia* to describe this unusually strong proficiency (from the Greek, *eu* = good). Thus, the eusemic child is the one so highly skilled in the use of expressive and receptive nonverbal language that he or she is able to move with ease socially and can establish and maintain friendships effectively. In contrast to the dyssemic child, eusemic children may be described as follows:

- tend to feel good about themselves, will describe themselves as happy and satisfied

- have high self-esteem

- are perceived by others as comfortable with themselves regardless of whether they have few or many close friends

- tend to be the ones chosen to be part of a group and often to be the leader of the group

- see a connection between what they do and what happens to them; do not often offer explanations or excuses having to do with luck, fate, or the impact of powerful others

- generally are not anxious or nervous

- use nonverbal expressions that are most often positive or happy; smile a great deal

- can stay focused on tasks

- seem to know what is appropriate to say to peers and adults in social situations

- will often offer to help beyond their own work

- are seen by teachers as competent and trustworthy.

There is no firm number of indicators for defining eusemia. However, the greater the number of indicators that apply to a child, the more likely it is that the child is successful in processing nonverbal social information.

Dyssemia and eusemia are both relatively rare. Ten percent of the population have nonverbal language deficits serious enough to cause social rejection. Similarly, only a small number of people could be described as eusemic. The vast majority of children and adults will fall somewhere between the two extremes. This book addresses the potential of that majority of children who have developed *some* skills in nonverbal communication, but who have not yet achieved a sense of mastery in the language of relationships. It is essential for parents and teachers to understand, however, that the information and exercises in this book are intended to improve their children's nonverbal skills—the achievement of *all* the characteristics of eusemia listed above is an unrealistic goal.

The more children know about nonverbal language, the better they will do in relating to others; even moderate improvements, then, should be seen as valuable and worthy of pursuit. Further information and tips are contained in the following chapter so that you can conduct an informal evaluation of your child's current nonverbal language skills. Once you have evaluated your child's level of nonverbal communication abilities, you will be ready to help him or her to maximize those skills.

2

ASSESSING NONVERBAL SKILLS

If you wanted to assess your children's verbal language skills, you might listen to their speech, ask for their understanding of a passage they have read, or perhaps read a sample of their writing. As you did these things, you would examine word selection, spelling, pronunciation, and meaning. Because of all of the formal and informal training that we as adults have received in verbal language use, you would know what to look for. However, when it comes to nonverbal language, most adults are usually only slightly more aware of its importance than children. Thus, a first step in assessing your children's developmental levels is becoming familiar with the structure of nonverbal communication—the six channels described in Chapter One.

The first and most important tool for any parent is an awareness of what to look for and where to look for it.

If you can accurately estimate your children's current levels of expressive and receptive nonverbal language abilities, you will be taking the first major step in developing a plan for their social growth. Parents can teach young children verbal language skills without any formal training; in the same manner, they can informally, yet effectively, estimate and improve a child's nonverbal language abilities without professional knowledge. Indeed, the first and most important tool for any parent is an awareness of what to look for and where to look for it. When you become aware of the components of nonverbal language, you will be able to observe consciously what you normally might not notice. Then you will be in a good position to use your common sense to evaluate your children's level of nonverbal language development and take the next step: determine the relation of language development to the child's age.

At this point you might be saying: "Wait a minute, I'm not a professional. How am I supposed to know what is age-appropriate?" We suggest that you think of how many times you have said to a child, "Act your age," or to another adult, "She's only three, she'll grow out of that." In these and other instances, we are applying an implicit and culturally shared set of standards which relate age and situation to appropriate behavior. We use the same sort of age-related and shifting standards when we accept thumb-sucking in toddlers, but not in grade-school children.

Be confident! Sometimes your individual assessment of a child's abilities might be a bit (rarely very far) off, but chances are that if you, other family members, and your child's teacher agree in your estimation of his or her nonverbal skills, you are probably right on target.

Before you begin any assessment or remediation activities, it is *vital* to let children know what you are doing, especially if they seem to be experiencing some confusion about social relationships. Discuss openly what you are trying to learn about; begin forming in their minds a link between nonverbal language patterns and the development of friendships. Form a partnership; be a tutor. Be sure that you exhibit the same degree of patience and support that you show when the child is working on verbal skills. You are merely adding a new dimension to the learning that comes out of good parent-child relationships.

INFORMAL METHODS OF ASSESSMENT

With a positive attitude and a little old-fashioned ingenuity, you can make assessment pleasant and fun. In assessing your child's receptive abilities, you will find that the television is one simple, informal, and useful device that children will accept with little or no problem. Select a satisfactory program showing substantial interactions among children and adults (we have found "Sesame Street" and various daytime dramas to be good choices), turn off the sound, and ask your child to tell you what is going on by simply watching the picture. Every so often, turn up the volume to determine your child's accuracy. Focus on the different types of nonverbal communication separately and in combination with each other: What do the characters' facial expressions indicate? How about when facial expressions are combined with their postures?

Conversely, you can have the children face away from the TV and listen only to the sound while trying to describe what they think is going on visually. If the characters are shouting, what should their facial expressions indicate? What posture might a whispering character take? These are just some of the easy and enjoyable ways to use television to find out how adept your child is at reading nonverbal cues.

Additional assessments of receptive skills can be made by observing people interacting in various places and asking the children to tell you what they think is going on. For example, people-watching in shopping malls can provide a wealth of social exchanges to discuss. A child's ability to explain what is happening will tell you how adept that child is at reading nonverbal social information. Have your child watch people sitting in food courts or restaurants; see if the child can guess how those people are feeling and what their relationships are. You can also view groups of individuals as they move through the mall and ask the child to infer what, if any, relationships these people might share.

Estimating expressive nonverbal abilities may be an even easier task than determining the receptive ones. While doing this, the most important thing is for you to be aware of how your child sends nonverbal language signals. There are many opportunities to watch your child interact with others or respond to situations (at birthday parties, in arguments, or while viewing a sports event, movie, or television show). Knowing what feelings are appropriate to the event or interaction, you can assess whether the child is accurately expressing those feelings. Through these observations, you will become aware of how easily others might interpret how your child is feeling.

If you are having trouble reading the child's emotions, chances are that others are too. Or, if you find that the child's nonverbal language does not reflect his or her probable internal state—for example, if while playing and having a good time at a birthday party, a child's expression is angry or sad—you will know that others are likely to misinterpret the child's facial expressions.

If you have a Polaroid camera or a video recorder, you can be a bit more systematic about your observations. Ask children to show certain emotions and record their attempts; this photographic record can help you decide if they have difficulties in expressing feelings nonverbally. Remember, however, that this kind of technique is reactive; children will react to being photographed and may not show the kind of nonverbal communications that they usually do—they may be "camera shy" or "performing" rather than behaving naturally. Try to reduce this possibility by making the picture-taking part of a game, perhaps with a group of children, or by having the child also take pictures of you. You can also photograph the child when he or she is unaware that you are doing so, perhaps on the playground or at a party. These general observational assessments will help you evaluate your child's nonverbal communication processing abilities.

SYSTEMATIC METHODS OF ASSESSMENT

Most of the time, the informal observation techniques described here and in Part Two will yield enough information for you to determine your child's level of nonverbal language development. Careful informal observation—especially if you know where to look and if you seek agreement from others who also know your child—can often be just as effective, and certainly less expensive and disruptive, than the formal procedures described in this section. However, there are instances in which the informal methods are unsatisfactory, either because the information is inconclusive or because the patterns of behavior you are looking for seem far too complex. In such cases, more systematic methods of observation may be useful.

Determine how concrete you need your observations to be in order to accurately assess—and then improve—your child's nonverbal communication. Formal observation will allow you to be more certain about the actual levels of nonverbal language development and to be more precise in planning nonverbal practice and other learning experiences. Remember that any of these procedures may be modified and adapted to your needs as you see fit.

Formal observation should include systematic focus on the child's abilities to receive and express nonverbal social information. However, few tests for this are available at this time. Tests of auditory and visual perception that determine the basic ability of children to hear and see accurately may not always involve the specific abilities of processing social cues, such as the emotional meaning of facial expression and tone of voice. *If you do seek the help of a professional, we suggest that you explain your concerns and work with that person to develop individualized tests.* Keep in mind that any informal or formal efforts to evaluate nonverbal communication skills should include observations of your child's abilities to:

- discriminate among nonverbal cues

- identify the emotions presented in nonverbal communication

- express emotions through various nonverbal channels

- apply nonverbal information to interpret what is happening in diverse conversations.

While our systematic method of assessing nonverbal language skills was developed for use by mental health professionals and classroom teachers, parents may easily adapt it for their own more informal use. The procedures are based to a significant degree on the work of Esther Minskoff and Johnson and Myklebust, and on our own work with teachers, parents, and children. This chapter provides an overview of the basic components of the systematic approach. We want to emphasize that these procedures can and should be modified to fit the needs and existing skills of a particular child.

All of the procedures in this book are based on theory, research, and experience suggesting that:

- children and adults who have trouble processing nonverbal information tend to have problems in relating to others, while children and adults who are skilled in the use of nonverbal language tend to succeed in interpersonal relationships.

- nonverbal social processing skills can be accurately assessed through both formal and informal means and can be taught with appropriate instructions.

- improved nonverbal processing skills translate into better interpersonal relationships and social success.

DANVA

We have constructed our own formal assessment test, the Diagnostic Analysis of Nonverbal Accuracy (DANVA), which focuses on the major nonverbal communication channels. While the DANVA is designed as a formal assessment instrument for use by professionals, you may find it helpful to modify some of the procedures for use in your own informal observations of your child.

The DANVA is composed of nine subtests—four to measure the ability to understand nonverbal communication and five to measure the ability to send nonverbal information. These tests cover the most frequently used channels of nonverbal communication: tone of voice, facial expressions, personal space, postures, and gestures. The subtests use the most commonly encountered emotions—anger, fear, happiness, and sadness—to measure the abilities to receive and send nonverbal information.

- **Understanding Facial Expressions:** This test assesses children's abilities to identify emotions being communicated by the facial expressions of adults and children. Twenty-four photographs of adults and twenty-four of children depict happy, sad, angry, and fearful facial expressions at either a high or a low level of emotional intensity. The photographs are shown one at a time, for a full second, to the child, who then can match the photo with one of the four emotions. Older children can write down their own answers; younger children may say their answers and have the examiner write them down. As an aid to the child, the four emotions can be displayed on a strip of paper. The facial expressions also can be presented via slide projector for group testing. Each slide is shown for one second, followed by a blank screen. While the screen is blank, the children can write down their answers.

- **Sending Facial Expressions:** This test consists of eight trials. The child should be sitting in a comfortable chair, ten feet away from a video camera. The examiner then reads one of eight descriptive situations and asks the child to express a proper emotion. For example, the examiner would say, "You have received a birthday present that you have always wanted. You feel happy. Show me a happy face." The child's expression is then videotaped. There are two descriptive examples for each of the four basic emotional states (anger, fear, happiness, and sadness). Rating scales that range from one (not accurate) to three (very accurate) are used to judge the child's abilities to convey the appropriate emotions. Important here is the intensity of the emotion as well as the accuracy; it is possible for a child to correctly communicate a particular emotion while overstating or understating that emotion by projecting an improper intensity.

- **Understanding Gestures:** Photographs show a model using gestures that reflect the four basic emotions (anger, fear, happiness, and sadness). Each of the four emotions is represented by three photographs (there are twelve photographs in all). The photographs are shown for one second, and the child must indicate which emotion is being expressed through the particular gesture. The examiner can also use slides to administer the test to groups.

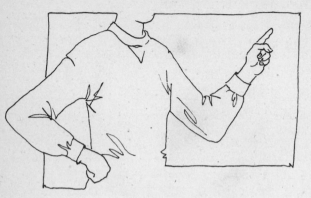

- **Sending Gestures:** In this test, there are twelve trials—three for each of the four basic emotions. The child, seated in a comfortable chair ten feet from a video camera, is instructed to use only his or her hands and arms to send a particular emotion (anger, for example). The child's gestures are videotaped and rated for accuracy.

- **Understanding Tone of Voice:** There are adult and child forms of this subtest. In the adult receptive test, there are twenty-four instances in which the sentence, "I am going out of the room now, but I will be back later," is said by either a male or a female. The sentence is recited to reflect either high- or low-intensity emotions— happy, sad, angry, or fearful. The child listens to the sentence and indicates which emotion is being communicated. The examiner can print the four emotions on a piece of paper to remind the subject of the choices.

    In the child-appropriate form of the tone of voice test, there are sixteen trials in which a child says the following sentence, "I am going out of the room now, and I will be back later." Each time, the model varies the voice tone to reflect one of the four basic emotions. Once again, the subject listens and chooses the appropriate emotion.

- **Sending Tone of Voice:** There are eight trials in this test. The child is seated in a comfortable chair next to a tape recorder's microphone (or video camera with a microphone). The examiner then hands the child a piece of paper upon which is printed, in block letters, the following sentence: "I am going to get my bike now and go for a ride." The child is given time to practice reading the sentence. The examiner then describes one of eight situations. The child responds by reading the sentence into the microphone, inflecting the appropriate words, and expressing the appropriate emotion for the described situation. For example, the cue could be, "You have found out that you have won a prize in a contest. You feel happy. Say the sentence in such a way that you sound happy." There are two trials for each of the four emotions. The recordings are subjected to ratings similar to those used to rate facial expressions and gestures.

- **Understanding Postures:** In this test, there are twelve photographs of a person showing various postures (care is taken to hide the face of the person portraying the posture). The postures reflect the four basic emotions (anger, fear, happiness, and sadness). Each emotion is represented by three slides. The photographs are shown for one second, and the child must state which emotion is being expressed through posture. Slides can be used to test groups; the slide is only shown for one second.

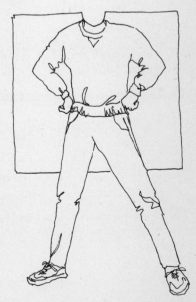

- **Sending Postures:** In this test, the child is read various stories that reflect happy, sad, angry, and fearful events, and his or her postural responses are videotaped and then rated for accuracy. At the end of each story, the child is told whether the event was happy, sad, angry, or fearful, and makes a posture that reflects that feeling. There are high- and low-intensity stories for each emotion.

- **Sending Personal Space:** To measure personal space, the Comfortable Interpersonal Distance Scale is used.

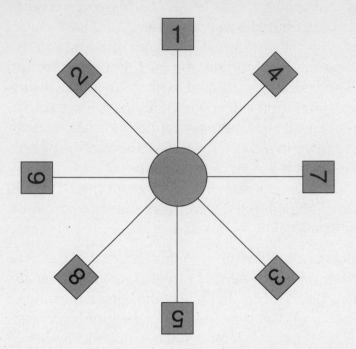

figure 2.1
Comfortable
Interpersonal
Distance Scale

People taking the test are given a piece of paper with a representation of a room on it similar to that shown in figure 2.1, above. From the center of the room, eight lines of equal length (eighty millimeters) radiate out in a circle.

Children taking the test are asked to imagine that they are standing in the center of the room and that each line leads to a different door. The examiner asks them to imagine that they are facing door 1 (the number at the top of the page), describes an imaginary person at that door, then says that the described person is going to walk toward the center of the room (where the child is "standing"). Children are instructed to make a mark on the line where they would like the imaginary person to stop. After making the mark, they are asked to imagine turning to the right and facing door 2. The tester then describes a different imaginary person at that door.

The examiner can use all eight doors and describe any sorts of individuals desired. For example, the person could be a stranger who is the same age and same gender as the child taking the test, or the described individual could be the president of the United States. For the DANVA the following individuals were described:

- a stranger who is the same age and sex as you

- a stranger who is the same age and opposite sex as you

- a stranger who is five years younger than you and the same sex

- a stranger who is five years older than you and the same sex

- your best friend

- your mother

- a schoolteacher who is a stranger to you

- the president of the United States.

The interpersonal distance between the center point and the marks made for each described individual is measured. The distances chosen for the imaginary people are then compared to the average distances chosen by a large group of the child's peers. This test tells the examiner whether the child's distances are greater or less than the norm.

When used by professionals who have access to the DANVA norms, scores from the nine subtests can produce a profile of a child's nonverbal processing abilities. DANVA norms, based upon the testing of several thousand children, allow for the evaluation of children's performances as compared to those of their peers. For example, the average fifth grader can recognize twenty-nine out of a possible thirty-two facial expressions correctly. If the child we test is a fifth grader, and he or she correctly identifies nineteen faces, we know the child's performance is much below that of other fifth graders. Further, if the person we test is twenty-one years old and can only identify nineteen faces correctly, we know that this person is performing at a level much below that of fifth graders, let alone that of adult peers.

The results of formal educational research are often greatly modified by teachers who apply that research to classroom situations. Thus, it should come as no surprise that there is often a difference between the formal theoretical foundation for an approach to teaching social success and the application of those concepts in the real lives of children. Teachers and parents can use the DANVA as a guide as long as they follow these suggestions:

- Learn how and why nonverbal language is related to social success.

- Discover where to look for evidence of nonverbal language strengths and weaknesses.

- Develop an individualized, entertaining, supportive, and effective teaching and learning program. From there, let your common sense, intuition, and love for your children be your guides.

3

TEACHING AND REMEDIATION

Maneuvering through social situations is akin to paddling down a rapid river where rocks or trees may crop up in the water at any moment. If we "read" these obstacles correctly and have the wherewithal to respond to them appropriately, we can continue our journey unscathed; if we don't see them or don't know how to navigate around them, we run a high risk of capsizing. To successfully interact, we must be able to "read" nonverbal language correctly and to respond to it appropriately. Further, the signs and cues that we produce for others must be clear and decipherable and must accurately reflect what we are trying to say.

Most children are not, and need not be, eusemic. All children, however, need opportunities and experiences that will help them to develop their nonverbal language skills to the best of their abilities. Like most adults, each child will grow to be really proficient in some areas of nonverbal communication, average in other areas, and downright weak in a few. To optimize social success, we need to help children learn where their strengths are and encourage them to rely on those strengths. At the same time, we need to teach them what their weaknesses are and how to transform them into advantages.

Once areas of strength and weakness have been identified and a decision is made to develop a child's nonverbal language abilities to the fullest, the process of teaching and remediation begins. Before starting any remediation activities, *it is important to discuss your intentions explicitly and directly with your child.* Too often, children are asked to complete tasks with no explanation of why they are being asked to do them and no understanding of what benefits will come from their mastery. If you are aware of specific problems you wish to improve by remediation, explain the problems to the child. Do this without assigning any blame, but instead projecting a positive outlook. The remediation can be portrayed as a game or as exercises or homework—the approach depends on the individual adult and child.

The teaching of nonverbal language skills should occur in a lighthearted, helpful, and supportive climate. Since children are attempting to learn associations that may be new and possibly difficult for them, it is important for the tutor to try to create an atmosphere in which failures are accepted and successes are reinforced. In other words, the process of learning should be fun. Depending on their age and their specific strengths and weaknesses, children will differ in the speed at which they learn nonverbal social processing skills. Do not rush the learning process. Starting with small tasks and making sure that the child feels comfortable is more important than progressing at a fast pace. After a new activity or series of activities, make sure that children have grasped and processed the information before moving on.

The teaching of nonverbal language skills should occur in a lighthearted, helpful, and supportive climate.

Developing a child's nonverbal language skills is not a process that can occur in a short time. It is, rather, a long-term one in which children and parents or teachers work together and have fun. As we have said, just as we must learn many thousands of words and expressions to master our verbal language, we must also learn to recognize and interpret many signs and symbols in order to master our nonverbal language.

It is extremely important to concentrate first on exactly "where the child is" in this process of mastering nonverbal language before you start any remediation program. The assessment chapter just before this one and the specific channel discussions to follow explain how to best gauge your child's nonverbal abilities.

Parents and teachers can help a child learn to associate particular feelings with particular nonverbal behaviors by explaining the connection between them. This goal is consistent with the recommendations made by Johnson and Myklebust, who believe that a child needs to establish these associations by direct learning. The more often informal conversations center or touch upon the hundreds of nonverbal cues both received and produced each day, the more sensitive children will become to these cues and the more effective they will be in utilizing them in establishing successful social relationships. If parents put forth even 25 percent of the effort that they put forth in cultivating and refining verbal skills into teaching nonverbal language, they would see major improvements in their children's social behavior; if teachers became more systematically involved in the nonverbal learning process, they could help their students achieve great improvements in social success.

It is important that a spirit of fun and enthusiasm pervade all activities directed at optimizing the development of nonverbal language, but particular care should be taken with home-based activities. If children become tense or if parents often let their frustrations show, the process of learning can be defeated. Patience over time will be rewarded with children's improved skills and greater social success. When frustration looms, think of how much time and how much practice has gone into every child's verbal language skills!

FEATURES OF THE TEACHING AND
REMEDIATION PROGRAMS

The purpose of teaching and remediation is to develop or improve skills. All of the activities in this book are designed to be:

- **systematic**: to teach in an organized way that makes sense to the pupil.

- **ordered or graded**: to disclose increasingly complex information.

- **cumulative**: to build up and thoroughly explore each learning process before progressing to the next level.

- **multisensory**: to integrate visual, auditory, and tactile modalities.

- **sympathetic**: to instill the confidence in each individual that a tutor understands his or her specific difficulties and wants to help.

The following suggestions will facilitate the teaching and remediation processes for all students, no matter their level of nonverbal communication skill.

- Maintain the child's interest level.

- Set goals. Work on one area of improvement at a time.

- Give individual attention as frequently as possible. Encourage the student to ask many questions.

- Deliver new information more than once. Review and reinforcement are necessary.

- Help the student to relate new skills to past experience.

- Be positive, and work on building the student's self-esteem.

- Allow children to learn any way they can, using any tools available.

- Practice.

- Practice.

- Practice!

Ideally the teaching environment should be a specified place which the child learns to associate with the remediation exercises. If creating such an area is not possible, then the lesson itself should consistently follow a recognizable routine which the child associates with the remediation. No matter the location, the teaching environment—given the constraints of available space—should be orderly, reliable, and inspiring of trust.

Each chapter in Part Two of this book concludes with exercises that any parent or teacher can use with individual children. When you and your children practice these exercises, you are both assessing their abilities and improving their knowledge and performance of each of the channels discussed. These informal remediation methods are all most children will need to improve their nonverbal communication skills. If you wish to practice any or all of these channels further, or if your child seems to be having difficulty with any of these elements, Chapters Eleven and Twelve offer further informal and formal approaches to improving nonverbal communication.

A little preparation at the outset can go a long way in making the activities suggested in this book more organized and consequently much more fun!

To fully benefit from the remediation process, the child must understand pertinent vocabulary; use the key words listed below to assess your child's understanding of the necessary vocabulary.

Key Words:

- analyze
- cause
- classify
- communicate
- compare
- detail
- different
- effect
- emotion
- expression
- feature
- language
- message
- nonverbal
- observe
- organize
- receive
- send
- similar
- verbal
- zone

Working with children—using their own words where possible—establish verbal definitions for each of the above and record them in a "help pack" or personal dictionary for reference.

Do not worry that some words may appear very difficult for a younger child. With your expertise and mediation, you will be able to help a child grasp even the most complex concepts. Begin by asking, "What do you understand about the word ____?" and give a sample sentence which contains the word. Some words with several meanings will require longer discussion, for example, the word "communication." Once you explain the concept, discuss with the child the various methods of communicating, such as verbally, nonverbally, in written form, etc. The more you discuss words with children, the better their understanding of them will be.

The following example of children traveling on a bus through the country with their mothers should show the value of your efforts more clearly.

Kevin looks out of the bus window and asks, "What is that?" His mother looks and replies, "It is a cow." Kevin now has a label for the object, but since his mother has merely handed him a brief answer, he has no further knowledge of the animal. It is unlikely that he has formed an internal picture of what constitutes a cow. This child was merely a *passive* recipient of information.

Jessica asks her mother the same question. Her mother replies with more questions of her own. "How many legs does it have?" "What color is it?" "How big is it?" When Jessica has answered these questions and asked some more questions like "What does it eat?" or "What sound does it make?", the mother explains, "It is a cow."

Jessica had to work for her answer, drawing together details until she had a complete picture. She is now able to create a visual image of a cow with relative ease, and has more than one reference point from which to retrieve the information. Her mother mediated this learning experience. This child was an *active* participant in the learning process.

The active participation of the child is the goal of all of the exercises in this book.

If you believe that your child has not reached his or her fullest potential in the use of nonverbal language, there are steps you can take to help him or her develop their skills.

LOOKING AHEAD

It is important to note that we are not suggesting that all children must act in exactly the same way in all situations—we are not prescribing conformity of behavior. Rather, we are proposing that in order to communicate effectively, children must know how to "say" what they wish to say. For example, all children don't have to enjoy eating spinach, but they should all be familiar with the word "spinach." The precise messages children wish to send nonverbally—just as the precise ideas they would wish to communicate in words—are entirely up to them and will vary from child to child and situation to situation.

In order to achieve socially successful relationships, children must know how to communicate clearly and how to read other people's nonverbal messages as easily as they understand their words. Armed with a new awareness and a wide array of nonverbal skills, young people will find that social relationships are much less mysterious, confusing, and stressful.

The next section of this book will explain the six areas of nonverbal communication and show you ways to determine your child's strengths and weaknesses in each area. Each channel chapter concludes with informal, at-home exercises for assessing nonverbal proficiency and then for improving nonverbal skills. These exercises can be used as needed. Many of the activities suggested—trips to shopping malls, use of TV and videotapes, etc.—serve the dual purpose of evaluation and practice for improvement. You should perform the activities described in the upcoming chapters in an atmosphere of partnership, cooperation, and fun, and you should be sure to make the child aware of what you are doing and why.

Once you have determined the areas of relative strengths and weaknesses in your child's expressive and receptive nonverbal language, your next step is setting up a program to maximize his or her potential. For some children, informal, short-term practice and activities (such as those included in the six channel chapters) may be all that is necessary to head them in the direction of improvement and growth. For other youngsters, a more systematic, long-term effort might be the better approach. Part Three features systematic approaches to teaching and remediation, including information geared to children in a classroom setting and a full nonverbal curriculum. Whether you choose an informal or systematic approach, prioritize your targeted areas from the outset and progress slowly so that your child can recognize success in achieving these goals.

How to Begin Assessment, Teaching, and Remediation

These guidelines will help you begin the assessment, teaching, and remediation of your child.

⇨ Using the A to Z lists included at the back of this book as a reference, identify those emotions, gestures, or postures you want to focus on with your child. Add any others you feel are important to your situation.

⇨ Begin to collect pictures of a variety of people (young and old, male and female, etc.), portraying a variety of facial expressions, postures, and gestures. You can find happy (and occasionally sad) photographs in most magazines. Look through national and local newspapers for good examples of negative nonverbal behavior. Your family photograph albums can also be excellent resources. Select photographs which have strong memories or emotional meaning attached, as such connections often make it easier for the child to understand the nonverbal signals in the photos.

Remember that nonverbal behaviors do not occur in isolation, so many photographs may be useful for several nonverbal exercise sections. For example, some photographs you intend to use for facial expressions may also work for exercises on postures, gestures, or objectics.

⇨ Purchase some brightly colored construction paper or poster board and a set of felt pens for making interesting charts and tables.

⇨ Photocopy and laminate pages 178 and 179 so that your materials will be reusable.

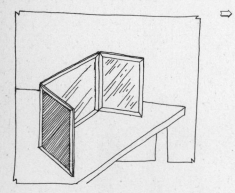

figure 3.1

⇨ Acquire a three-way mirror (a lighted, folding makeup mirror works well) or make one easily and cheaply by visiting a glass store or warehouse and having a mirror cut to size. Cut two pieces 8 inches x 11$\frac{1}{2}$ inches. Cut one piece in half so that you have two 8 inch by 5$\frac{3}{4}$ inch pieces. Use duct tape (available at any hardware store) to connect the three pieces of glass along the shorter sides and cover the sharp outer edges (see figure 3.1, left).

Part Two

The Parts of Speech of Nonverbal Language

4

Paralanguage

Nearly one-third of the emotional meaning invested in conversations is carried by paralanguage, a term that refers to the forms of nonverbal communication that can be heard. How people sound when they speak is a very important indicator of how they feel. The ability to pick up the feelings behind the words is an important social skill that is crucial to the development and maintenance of relationships. An important, parallel social skill is the ability to express accurately how we feel by the use of appropriate sounds.

Paralanguage refers to all the aspects of sound which accompany words or act independently of them to communicate emotion. Included here are such things as tone, loudness, intensity of voice, and sounds uttered between or instead of words such as humming and whistling. Often the importance of paralanguage is obscured when we have access to visual nonverbal information like facial expressions, postures, gestures, and so on. However, much as watching television with the sound turned down accentuates visual signals, communicating on the telephone enhances our dependence on paralinguistics. This fact makes some people uncomfortable on the phone, especially

P*ARALANGUAGE refers to all the aspects of sound which accompany words or act independently of them to communicate emotion.*

those of us who are not adept at this kind of nonverbal communication.

Parents and teachers are often much more aware than children of the presence or absence of paralanguage skills. When children are good at paralinguistic expression, they can be encouraged and helped to become even better. When they manifest patterns that can cause problems (this even includes such "simple" things as excessive throat clearing, whining, and abrasive laughs) they must be helped to modify their communications. Sensitive, well-placed suggestions regarding the problem pattern are not always successful but nevertheless necessary. When given in private by someone whom the child trusts, such suggestions can begin the process of awareness and learning that can ultimately have dramatic effects on the interpersonal and emotional worlds of youngsters.

There are four aspects of paralanguage that are important to the communication of our feelings:

- tone of voice

- nonverbal sound patterns

- rate of speech

- emphasis and variation in speech.

TONE OF VOICE

Sometimes the importance of what we say is outweighed by *how* we say it. Our tone of voice makes it possible to say the words, "I hate you," yet communicate "I love you," and vice versa. Because responsiveness to tone of voice is so basic, it seems to take precedence over verbal communication whenever the two differ. The ability to accurately read or express meaning through tone of voice may be the most important aspect of nonverbal language.

We know how to respond to tone of voice long before we

are able to react to the meanings of words. Consider how "Baby Richie" responded.

Six-month-old Richie and his parents visited friends. His parents were very excited about little Richie's intellectual abilities and liked to show him off. The major measure of his "genius" was that even at his early age, Richie could understand the meanings of words. To prove this, his father looked at him, and with a big grin and wide-open eyes, asked, "How big is Richie?" Richie responded to the question with a "so big" sign with his hands and arms. His parents were pleased with their brilliant son, but what they had failed to realize was that the words, "How big is Richie" were always said in a specific, rhythmic, singsong way, and in a particular tone of voice. Richie was responding to the nonverbal cues, not the words. The family friends proved this when they said "Pizza pie and ice cream" with the same emphasis and tone of voice. Richie responded with his popular "so big" gesture.

Tone of voice is a prime communicator of emotion. To know the emotional state of those with whom we interact is to be in touch with them at the most complete and basic level; to be unaware of others' feelings is to invite confusion and turmoil into interpersonal relationships. There are many examples of instances in which just the right tone of voice has determined the outcome of an important moment.

For example, consider the use of tone of voice by a fourth-grade teacher we once observed. This young woman was incredibly skilled in using her tone of voice to guide and control her classroom. When students were busily working, all of her comments were said in a gentle and upbeat manner; when someone began to act up a bit, we could trace a parallel shift in her voice tone designed to "correct" the course of the lesson. All good teachers can do this; conversely, many teachers who have trouble managing their classrooms cannot.

Cognitive conflict is an important concept related to tone of voice. *Cognitive conflict* is a puzzling mismatch between tone of voice and content of communication. For example, if someone angrily yells "Have a good day," that person's tone of voice is in conflict with the verbal message; the speaker is thus sending two opposite messages at the same time.

Sarcasm also falls under the header of tone of voice. When someone uses a sarcastic tone, there is a discrepancy between what the person's words mean and what his or her tone of voice indicates. Explain this concept to your child carefully (include the fact that sarcasm is generally disrespectful, hurtful, or insincere). Reinforce the point that when the children suspect sarcasm, they must observe other nonverbal clues to ascertain the speaker's true meaning; in other words, explain that words cannot always be taken literally. *Sarcasm is likely to be a very difficult concept for the child to grasp.*

NONVERBAL SOUND PATTERNS

Very young children use a number of sounds and noises to communicate their needs and desires to adults. Such vocalizations aren't used as often by older children, but they occur frequently enough in conversations to make life difficult for a child who cannot express or understand the meaning of sound patterns.

The nonword "mmmmmmm" can indicate either a positive or a negative feeling, while a hissing sound usually indicates a clear dislike. In addition to using nonverbal vocalizations to communicate likes and dislikes, parents and teachers often use other sounds to guide the behavior of children. However, success in guiding children through nonverbal sounds depends on children's understanding of the meaning of these sounds. The following incident reveals the importance of understanding nonword vocalizations.

> Some schoolchildren were playing on a fenced playground near an open gate which led to the street. Four children broke off from the main group and walked toward the gate as if they were going to go through it. A teacher was standing near the gate reading, and she noticed the children's approach out of the corner of her eye. Without looking up she uttered, "mmmm-mmmmmm-mmmmmmmm," with each "mmm" being higher in pitch than the last, and with the last being said in a sort of singsong tone. (We hope you know what we are describing; to most of us it means, "You'd better stop and think about what you're going to do!") As a tribute to the power of such sounds, three of the four children stopped in their tracks; however, the fourth child kept right on going and the teacher had to run after her.
>
> In this case, the fourth child did not respond because she did not understand the meaning of the nonword sound the teacher used. If the teacher had been unaware of this child's difficulty in this area, she might have assumed that the child was defiant.

RATE OF SPEECH

It is not only the words or the tone of voice people use that communicate a message; the rate of their speech also conveys meaning. In an academic setting, a teacher who speaks rapidly may be perceived as being very well-prepared and knowledgeable. In other contexts, rapid speech can have an irritating or intimidating effect on others. Slow talking also affects listeners. The slow speech of a student giving a report may seem to signify insecurity or a lack of preparation; conversely, a parent's slow talking can have a soothing effect on a distraught child.

Most of us have a preferred rate of speech, but social effectiveness requires that we be flexible enough to speed up or slow down depending on whom we are talking with. Ideally, we should be able to modulate our rate of speech according to each situation and synchronize our rate of speech with that of others.

Ideally, we should be able to modulate our rate of speech according to each situation and synchronize our rate of speech with that of others.

As most people are unaware of other types of nonverbal language, they also lack awareness of their own rate of speech and the impression their rate of speech can make on others. Bob and Ray, a comedy team from the early days of radio, have a classic skit which makes this point nicely. In it, Ray has only a few minutes to interview Bob, who is a member of STOA—"Slow Talkers of America." The skit shows Ray's increasing tension as he waits impatiently for Bob's responses—each word comes in an agonizingly slow manner. Much of the comedy in the skit arises from Bob's inflexible expressive speech rate—his inability to speed up his speech to accommodate Ray. Bob also exhibits a receptive speech rate problem, however; he does not know how to properly read the cues indicating whose turn it is to talk. People like Bob will continue to talk in a slow monotone that allows no input from the other person; these are people who are also likely to interrupt others in the middle of a thought. These people cannot get "in sync," and as a result, their interactions tend to become more and more strained.

Synchronicity of rate of speech is important for positive and productive conversations. If people cannot achieve synchronicity, they should at least try to be aware of the differences between themselves and others.

EMPHASIS AND VARIATION IN SPEECH

Consider the following sentence: "I didn't say he took my money." These seven words present a potentially confusing message if one must interpret them without the benefit of cues such as word emphasis, tonal variation, and speech volume. To demonstrate our point, please read the sentence six times, each time emphasizing a different word. We have described below what changing the word emphasis does to the meaning of the sentence.

- <u>I</u> didn't say he took my money.
  (I didn't say it, someone else did.)

- I didn't <u>say</u> he took my money.
  (I didn't say it, but I believe it.)

- I didn't say <u>he</u> took my money.
  (He didn't take my money, someone else did.)

- I didn't say he <u>took</u> my money.
  (He didn't take it. I gave it to him or he found it.)

- I didn't say he took <u>my</u> money.
  (He didn't take my money, he took someone else's money.)

- I didn't say he took my <u>money</u>.
  (He didn't take my money, he took something else.)

In addition to word emphasis, variations in volume can also enhance what we are trying to say. People who speak without fluctuations, or in a *monotone*, are often perceived as dull and unresponsive. Most of us enjoy listening to people with variation and "lilt" in their voices; attend to this quality in successful public figures or other people you really enjoy being with and this point will become obvious.

If children can learn to vary their own speech emphases

appropriately and distinguish emphases in others' speech, clear and effective communication with many different kinds of people can result.

Paralanguage is different from the other forms of nonverbal communication we are discussing because the message is heard, not seen. If children can't hear and understand these signals, then they miss much of the nonverbal meaning that helps people interpret a situation correctly. An individual who can read these signs has a great social advantage.

PARALANGUAGE

Laying the Groundwork

⇨ Begin by explaining to children what paralanguage is. Help them by providing examples. Speak in a noticeable monotone at first. Then begin to change your voice to convey various emotions. Ask them to listen to you carefully and explain what they notice happening.

Tone of Voice

⇨ Discuss with children what they understand by "tone of voice." Give them examples of different tones of voice. Explain that tone most commonly identifies our emotion, and that tone of voice can alter the meaning of words.

⇨ Ask children to repeat a neutral sentence ("Mrs. Barton will arrive in a few minutes") in a tone of voice that reflects various emotions, such as sadness, happiness, anger, or excitement.

⇨ Read examples of short sentences in various tones of voice. Ask children to respond in what they consider an appropriate tone, or ask them to demonstrate how they would respond to a person perceived to be sad, happy, angry, or excited.

⇨ Say the same sentence several times, each time varying your tone. Ask children to describe the emotion they "read" in each tone of voice. Then ask them to describe appropriate or inappropriate reactions to that tone of voice.

⇨ Develop games in which children can exercise their voice tones and learn to gain control over them. For example, as a child is telling you a story or reading a paragraph, call out an emotion (sad, happy, angry, etc.) and require the child to shift to that voice tone without stopping the reading or talking. Conversely, read a passage and ask the child to identify your emotional state as you suddenly change your tone of voice.

⇨ Collect or make tapes of people with distinctive voices, such as famous actors playing good and bad characters. Let children listen to those voices and identify favorites, stating the reasons for their choices. Ask them what aspects of the voice they like or dislike.

⇨ Have a child stand behind a screen or with eyes closed, so that your facial expression, posture, and gestures are hidden. Ask the child to listen to your voice and identify the overall emotion conveyed by the tone of voice.

⇨ Have a child listen to his or her laugh and modulate it for different circumstances. You can record the child's laugh or simply listen to it.

⇨ Ask for examples of locations or situations where it is inappropriate to use a particular tone of voice.

INAPPROPRIATE TO USE A QUIET TONE
• busy places   • shopping mall   • emergency situations

INAPPROPRIATE TO USE A LOUD TONE
• library   • museum   • theater   • place of worship

⇨ Using the lotto board found in Part Four, play a game in which tone of voice and emotions are matched. Speak in a particular tone, and have the child identify the emotion that you are conveying.

⇨ Speak to your child in a sarcastic tone of voice, then ask him or her to describe the meaning of your tone of voice. Also ask the child how sarcasm made him or her feel. (Embarrassed? Angry? Confused?)

Nonverbal Sound Patterns

⇨ Ask your child the meaning of various sounds, such as:
  • cough (a warning)
  • "mmm" (nice taste)
  • "tut" (What you have said is rather silly)
  • "er" (I'm not sure, I'm thinking)

Explain that these sounds are used as a type of shorthand or "time saver." People would think it strange if, in certain situations, we used words rather than sending a nonverbal message. For example, if we said, "I'm thinking," rather than "Hmmmm," we might indicate irritation or frustration rather than simply taking a pause to think.

⇨ Play "paralanguage charades" in which emotional or personality characteristics such as friendliness, grumpiness, sadness, or trustworthiness are communicated through sounds only (using no actual words). For example, "harumph" could be expressed to signify grumpiness. Have the child both "send" as well as "receive" clues.

Rate of Speech

⇨ Tape your child talking normally in a natural situation. Count the number of words spoken in one minute to determine his or her normal rate of speech. Tape yourself talking with another adult. Ask the child to identify who is talking the fastest and who is talking the slowest. Generally, a child speaks faster than an adult female, who in turn speaks faster than an adult male. If your child speaks much faster than other children or much slower than adults, your child may have an unusual rate of speech.

⇨ Ask your child to consider what various rates of speech convey.

EMOTIONS OR MESSAGES CONVEYED BY SLOW SPEECH
- The speaker is comforting someone.
- The speaker is uncertain of his or her topic.
- The speaker is talking to a younger child or explaining something.

EMOTIONS OR MESSAGES CONVEYED BY FAST SPEECH
- The speaker is confident.
- The speaker is rushed.
- The speaker is nervous.
- There is an emergency.

⇨ Discuss the effects that various rates of speech can have on those receiving the information.

WHEN A PERSON IS TALKING UNUSUALLY FAST, THE LISTENER MAY
- miss vital information
- get lost and stop listening
- become frustrated

WHEN A PERSON IS TALKING SLOWER THAN THE NORMAL RATE, THE LISTENER MAY
- become bored and stop listening
- be insulted
- understand what is being said more easily

These examples show the importance of a correct rate of speech for particular situations; without an appropriate rate of speech, the meaning of our words might be wasted. Various emotions affect the rate at which we speak.

⇨ Ask children to match emotions with correct rates of speech.
- sad — slower rate
- happy — faster rate
- thoughtful — slower rate
- excited — faster rate

Emphasis in Speech

⇨ Explain to your child the meaning of the word "emphasis." Then create two sentences, one with relevance to home life ("Could you turn the music down?") and one with relevance to school life ("Put your books away."). Go through the sentences several times—emphasizing a different word each time—and ask the child what meaning is implied by the sentence each time. If the child has difficulty hearing the change in emphasis, grossly exaggerate the stressed word. Write the sentence down and ask the child to underline the word you have stressed.

⇨ Make use of audio books from the library to allow your child to hear how people use emphasis to indicate meaning and feelings. For younger children, look for tape and book sets; these sets allow children to follow the text as they listen to the monologue. They might even like to try reading along with the narrator.

⇨ Think up a bland sentence, like "The dog is outside." Ask the child to repeat the sentence with different emotional emphases and with various rates of speech. For example, saying "The dog is <u>outside</u>" very quickly might imply that we should hurry to bring the dog safely back inside. Saying "The dog <u>is</u> outside" rather slowly could imply that we are confident that the dog is no longer in the house, but back in the yard.

⇨ Now that the child understands the different aspects of paralanguage, ask him or her to make a list of public places where aspects of paralanguage would be especially important. For example:

• museum	• friends' homes	• restaurant	• classroom
• elevator	• lunchroom	• library	• place of worship
• school	• principal's office	• public transport	• cinema

Discuss each in turn and ask what the appropriate rate, tone, and intensity of speech would be in each situation.

⇨ Play lotto or invent a game in which cards with various nonverbal responses, paralanguage messages, and emotions written on them are used. Ask the child to select one card from each group and role-play a scene to you. Reverse roles to check the child's receptive skills.

⇨ Using the child's voice, your own voice, or a combination of both, prepare your own audio dictionary of voice tones that reflect various emotions and attitudes. See if accents affect the child's ability to detect nonverbal messages. Is the child better at detecting changes in female or male voices, or equally good at both?

5

FACIAL EXPRESSIONS

Most of the time, we are only vaguely aware of one another's rhythms, time usage, postures, gestures, and personal space. But faces always catch our attention. In fact, in any interaction, people spend more time looking at one another's faces than anywhere else. Doing so affords us valuable clues about one another's feelings and attitudes. People normally concentrate on one another's eyes, but other parts of the face also have the ability to communicate feelings; the mouth is a very important expressor—just think about the impact a smile or downturned mouth can make! The ability to read and express the subtleties of facial expression is one of the most important nonverbal skills. Because the ability to send and receive facial information accurately is central to communication, even slight problems in processing this information can cause significant interpersonal difficulties.

EXPRESSIVE AND RECEPTIVE FACIAL COMMUNICATION

As with the other types of nonverbal language, there are both expressive and receptive processes in facial communication. In almost every interaction, people exchange a steady stream of information about their attitudes and feelings

happiness

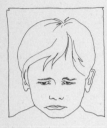

sadness

anger

fear

through their facial expressions. Effective human interaction depends upon the ability to accurately "send" feelings and attitudes through facial expressions and to accurately "read" those of others.

It is important to emphasize the development of skills in reading facial expressions. The majority of children should be able to identify and differentiate between happiness, sadness, anger, and fear in facial expressions. While "happiness" is the most easily identified nonverbal emotion, our research has shown that recognizing sadness, anger, and fear are more difficult and could require some extra practice. A common error among younger children is misreading a sad face as an angry one and then responding with avoidance or anger instead of the needed closeness and caring.

Early developmental errors, such as failing to learn to interpret certain facial expressions, can increase the likelihood of relationship confusions for children. If these errors are not corrected, they can be associated with adult relationship problems later on. One teacher told us of a boy who was unable to accurately "read" the stern face used by many teachers (and parents) to command a child's attention. On one or two occasions he looked up at her and asked, "Why are you standing there?" She became very angry with him until she realized that he really could not "read" the facial information she was sending.

But reading faces accurately is only half the story. People must also be able to produce facial expressions that reveal their intended feelings. We once studied a group of children who had significant relationship problems. We suspected that nonverbal communication skills, especially facial expressiveness, were involved. To test this possibility, we asked the children to "make faces" reflecting various feelings while we photographed them. We were surprised to find that, for several children, all the photographs looked essentially the same. The children in our study were unaware of it, but they were using similar facial expressions to communicate different emotions—actions sure to increase their chances of being misinterpreted and experiencing interpersonal frustration and apprehension.

The opposite is the case for socially successful children. They typically have the ability to vary their facial expressions in rapid and accurate ways. When they are feeling happy, they look happy; when they are feeling sad, they look sad. It is easy for others to relate to them because their facial expressions are accurate representations of their internal states—their feelings and attitudes. Relationships simply work better when based upon accurate sending and receiving of "signs" that represent our internal states.

Although we do not know the exact number of children who could benefit from increased practice in the communicative use of facial expressions, a study we completed on over a thousand children between the ages of six and ten suggests that there are more than just a few. We assessed the ability of these children to read as well as to send emotions accurately via facial expressions. We found that between 7 and 10 percent of these children had significant difficulty in either reading or producing specific emotional expressions and that an additional 7 to 10 percent were so proficient as to need little further work. We can assume from these figures that 80 percent of children can communicate adequately via facial expressions, but still have room for improvement in their abilities.

Besides showing the need for practice in nonverbal language use, the results of our study also indicated that children who were above average at processing facial information tended to be better adjusted. When we questioned teachers and other adults about what differentiated socially successful from socially rejected children, we found that they mentioned

The RESTING FACE *is the expression we "wear" when we are unaware of our expression.*

facial expression abilities time and time again. Adults frequently described socially successful children as "having a bright look" on their faces, as "smiling almost all the time," as "looking happy and satisfied," or as "having eyes that are alive."

THE RESTING FACE

The resting face is the most basic of facial expressions. Parallel to the "resting posture," to be discussed in Chapter Seven, the *resting face* is the expression we "wear" when we are unaware of our expression. Since other people do not know what is going on inside us, they interpret our facial expression as it appears to them, not as it feels to us.

Most people believe that their resting face is "neutral," showing neither positive nor negative emotions, but this is not the case. Most resting faces convey a low-intensity expression of one of the four primary emotions: happiness, sadness, anger, or fear. In the case of a young Japanese high school student, Miki, her resting face was quite pleasant and produced positive results.

resting face

Everyone seemed to like Miki from the first time she came to the school. There was something about her that attracted people, even those she did not know. It was obvious to the focused observer that Miki always kept a slight smiling expression on her face. Her mouth was a little upturned, accompanied by a version of "smiling eyes" (where eyebrows and cheeks are raised). In the same way that a smile or laugh can produce positive feelings in others, Miki's positive resting face produced pleasant sensations in those who looked at her.

Miki's likable facial expression greatly facilitated her quick acceptance and integration into a new school and environment.

Eye Contact and Smiling

Effective eye contact and the appropriate use of smiling are the two most frequently noted characteristics of socially successful children and adults. The successful use of facial expressions is well demonstrated by Wayne, a schoolchild who might have had a hard time with others due to his small size, but who utilized nonverbal language to the fullest. Wayne's smile lit up his entire face, and he smiled at everyone he met in the halls or passed on the street. No one could resist his grin, and almost everyone invariably returned it. Wayne's short stature faded into the background in comparison to his cheerful countenance.

A smile is one of the most easily recognized facial expressions and can dramatically influence the way others "read" and respond to the smiling individual. Because of this, the appropriate use of smiling should not be overlooked in any remediation program with your child.

Effective eye contact is necessary for the exchange of all visual, nonverbal information. Studies of interactions have shown that we look at the people we're communicating with more when we're listening to them than when we're speaking. During a conversation, for example, the average person spends 30 to 60 percent of the time looking at the other person's face. If we don't look at others this much while we're interacting with them, we can miss valuable interpersonal information. Stanford, a thirteen-year-old boy with expressive facial dyssemia, found out how poor eye contact can hinder peer relationships.

Stanford did not seem to know when he was supposed to speak in a conversation, he couldn't play games properly, and he had a knack for saying the wrong thing at the wrong time. Stanford was "out of sync" with his classmates and had few friends. After we observed Stanford, it became obvious that he simply did not look at others. When speaking, he averted his gaze either to the side or downward. Other people never knew whether or not Stanford was "receiving" their messages because he gave no properly timed visual cues. Further, when he spoke, others had difficulty determining when he was finished because he did not use the normal eye movements associated with the conclusion of a statement (the so-called "it's your turn" glance). Once Stanford became aware of the need to improve his eye contact, he was a willing partner in a program to help rectify this problem and improve his interpersonal interactions.

Stanford was neither expressing himself effectively through his nonverbal language nor receiving the complete message sent to him by others' nonverbal language.

--------------------------□--------------------------

This example shows how appropriate eye contact can improve the connection between people.

INTENSITY AND HORIZONTAL ZONING

Facially based interpersonal problems and successes can also be related to the intensity of facial expressions. If a child unknowingly uses the correct facial expression but with the wrong intensity (for example, laughing when smiling is appropriate or crying when a slightly sad expression is called for), others can be confused or respond incorrectly. The proper communication of emotional intensity occurs through a process called *modulation*. The ability to properly modulate ("turn up or turn down") nonverbal signs is a critical component of socially successful relationships. Thus, after what all agree to be a mildly amusing comment by a teacher or peer, children need to learn to respond with a moderate smile or limited laugh. If a child breaks into a great big grin and laughs uncontrollably, it will surely produce some puzzled glances and even embarrassed titters among his or her classmates.

While all the areas of nonverbal language are critical to social success, facial expressions along with paralanguage (discussed in Chapter Four) account for the greatest percentage of interpersonal impact, be that impact positive or negative. Phrases such as "his face dropped," "you should have seen the look on his face," "she looked down her nose at me," or "he was down in the mouth" emphasize the many ways our faces can express meaning. The face is the first place we look when we meet a new person. The face helps us to decide whether or not we think that a person is friendly or dangerous. If we send the wrong facial expression, we may be giving someone incorrect information about our feelings and our personality. For those able to read and produce these types of interpersonal cues, facial expressions provide an avenue to successful interactions and relationships.

FACIAL EXPRESSIONS

Laying the Groundwork

⇨ Ask children what they understand by the term "facial expression." Discuss how facial expressions convey emotions. Ask them why they think it matters that people are able to send and receive facial expressions accurately.

⇨ Discuss with children what they understand by the word "emotion." Remind the child that most of what we are feeling shows in our facial expressions. Using the A to Z of Emotions on pages 180-181, select the emotions that you consider most important for your child and ask him or her to give brief descriptions of those emotions. All you are testing here is the ability to understand the words—not the ability to express or receive that emotion correctly. Extend the discussion by asking for examples of circumstances which invoke each emotion.

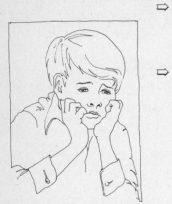

⇨ Develop an A to Z dictionary of facial expressions, pasting pictures of various expressions in a notebook or on index cards. Ask your child to label each expression.

⇨ Develop a set of facial expression stimuli by cutting out pictures of faces from magazines. Using these as facial "flash cards," ask the child to identify the emotion being portrayed. To vary this exercise, ask the child to act out a response to the expression on the flash card. Correctly acting out the emotion indicates a good understanding of the face. This exercise forces the child to both read and react to facial expressions.

Resting Face

⇨ Instruct the child, "Switch off your face and give me a neutral expression—one you believe shows no emotion." Take a photograph of this expression. If possible, catch the child unawares while watching television or reading and photograph them. You should notice that there is a difference between a child's artificial resting face and his or her actual resting face. Study the photograph with the child and discuss which, if any, of the four core emotions is identifiable. Ask the child, "Is the expression on your face positive and welcoming or is it negative and unwelcoming?"

⇨ Use a mirror to assist a child with a negative resting face to "lift" the expression and create a more positive resting face. This is likely to be a difficult problem to remediate because it requires a degree of reconditioning for the child. Concentrating on lifting all of the features on one's face when meeting people in public situations can work quite well; this internal reminder helps one gain an increased awareness of one's resting face.

⇨ Teach your child how to practice facial expressions (especially resting faces) by using a mirror. The child should practice major facial expressions (fear, anger, sadness, and happiness) for at least five minutes a day.

Using Eye Contact

⇨ Discuss with children the importance of maintaining eye contact when looking at a person, both to send an expression and to determine the expression of the other person. While talking to the child, try looking away or down frequently, and notice whether he or she picks up on it. Discuss the messages that good and poor eye contact convey.

POOR EYE CONTACT
- low self-esteem
- dishonesty
- fear
- disinterest

GOOD EYE CONTACT
- confidence
- sincerity
- interest
- knowledgeability

When you are asking children to consider eye contact, it is often useful to "bridge" to real-life experiences, that is, provide a link between what is being taught and its application and generalization to actual situations. For example, praise children for good eye contact during ongoing daily activities like eating lunch with friends or working on a task together.

If children do not maintain appropriate eye contact, then they are not maximizing their nonverbal language skills. If children are simply not yet aware of the importance of eye contact, then you may easily remediate the problem. If you find that a child has a persistent problem involving a lack of skill, however, you can use the following activities to encourage a steady gaze.

⇨ Sit down with your child and try to "stare each other down" for as long a period of time as both of you can manage. Record the time and try to improve on it. It is important to make it clear to the child that this *not* an appropriate way to look at people in general.

⇨ Have children practice fixing their gaze on a moving object (fixing the gaze on an object is a technique used by ballet dancers in motion). A pet or the face of a personality on television can work well as the moving object.

⇨ Ask children to study characters on television shows. Point out tactics used by particular personalities or characters. For example, news commentators and talk show hosts fix their gazes to make you feel that they are talking directly to you. Characters in soap operas often avoid eye contact when they are being devious or deceitful.

Horizontal Zoning

The whole face is not always involved in forming a particular emotional expression. Parts of the face play greater or lesser roles depending on which emotion is being depicted.

In order to help children understand how different parts of the face are used to express feelings, it is helpful to divide the face into three horizontal sections or zones (figure 5.1).

- Zone 1 — the forehead and eyes
- Zone 2 — the nose and cheeks
- Zone 3 — the mouth

Dividing facial expressions into these three groups is called *horizontal zoning*. Most facial expressions rely most heavily on Zone 1 (the forehead, eyebrows, and eyes), and on Zone 3 (the mouth). These are the parts of the face to which we pay the most attention and to which we respond the most strongly. If you cover the nose you will find that you lose very little in terms of expression, but if you cover the eyes you lose just about every necessary indication of expression.

Horizontal zoning is regarded as an important precursor to the acquisition of the skills necessary for automatic recognition of facial expressions. It should be repeated at the introduction of each new emotion. This procedure will take approximately twenty minutes when introducing a new emotion.

⇨ THE HORIZONTAL ZONING TECHNIQUE

You will need a three-sided mirror (see page 38), a large outline of a blank face (page 179), and pictures or photographs depicting the selected emotions.

1. Give the child the large blank face. Divide the face into three horizontal zones as shown in figure 5.1 and on page 64.

2. Place the mirror in front of the child. Place a picture showing a selected emotion in front of the child. Ask the child to produce the facial expression in the mirror. Point out on the picture and in the mirror: Zone 1 (forehead and eyes), then Zone 2 (nose and cheeks), and finally Zone 3 (mouth and chin). As you indicate each zone, use a blank card to cover the other zones.

3. Talk with the child about common features, those features by which we recognize and from which we identify a given emotion (for example, widely opened eyes or a tightly pursed mouth). Ask the child to look for such signals in the different zones. In some expressions, certain zones will have greater or lesser importance; for example, the middle zone often reveals the

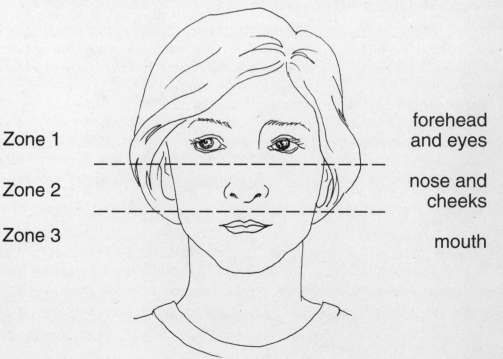

Zone 1   forehead and eyes

Zone 2   nose and cheeks

Zone 3   mouth

figure 5.1
Horizontal zones and features of the face

most subtle information (for example, flared nostrils can indicate anger). If a student is finding it difficult to discern any helpful features in Zone 2, concentrate on Zones 1 and 3.

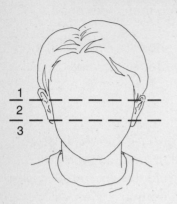

4. Ask the child to talk about the features shown in the picture as he or she draws them on the blank face. At each stage ask the student to mimic these key features in the mirror using a zoning template (a piece of paper used to block or isolate specific zones.) For example, as the child mimics an eye movement, conceal the nose and mouth with the card.

Concentrate initially on front views only, and progress to 45-degree and side profiles as the child becomes more familiar with the procedure.

Assistance is very important here. Many children may not know how to manipulate certain parts of their faces on cue, like raising or lowering their eyebrows. The parent or teacher should explain any errors and urge the child to verbally repeat any explanations given.

At this stage the student can be given a blank card for making a permanent record of the common features of emotions for future reference. For example, a beaming smile equals a high-intensity happy face, or wide-open eyes and mouth equals a high-intensity frightened face.

5. Ask the child to draw a face which shows the common features of the chosen expression on a card. The student or the tutor should record a written description of those features on the reverse of each card. For example, the features of a high-intensity happy face could be described like this: eyebrows relaxed; eyes crescent-shaped and curved upwards at the outer edges; mouth wide in a smile, showing teeth; upper lip straight; dimples around mouth.

6. If you have sufficient examples, repeat the procedures applied to high-intensity facial expressions with medium- and low-intensity expressions for the same emotion. Ask how the two or three intensities differ, but concentrate on the features that remain the same. If children feel the expressions are substantially different, allow them to create another reference face.

Once your child is familiar with the process, use the A to Z of Emotions on pages 180 and 181 to study more subtle facial expressions in a similar manner.

Mimicking

These exercises will help to raise your child's awareness of eye contact and the different messages that good and poor eye contact convey.

Children are good mimickers, observing and behaving by example. The following exercises help identify those facial expressions which are most difficult for an individual to manage. It is especially helpful when performed immediately after the horizontal zoning exercise (see pages 63-64), while the child's attention is focused. We recommend that you ask children to practice these exercises frequently.

Begin by using exclusively front-view portraits, progressing to 45-degree and side profiles when the child becomes more proficient at this procedure.

For these exercises you will need to select pictures showing the emotion(s) and intensities to be studied and a three-way mirror (see page 38).

⇨ Show the child a picture of a facial expression and clip it to the mirror in plain view. Ask the child to attempt to mimic in the mirror the expression shown on the picture. (Having the picture in front of the child will increase accuracy.) If the child makes an error, explain the mistake by highlighting the incorrect common feature. Ask the child to repeat your explanation.

⇨ Sit beside the student where you can both look into the mirror. Make a facial expression and ask the child to make a similar facial expression.

Using the same materials used in the mimicking exercise, ask your child to attempt different facial expressions from those represented in the picture.

⇨ Clip a picture to the mirror so that it faces the child. Then ask the child to attempt to make a facial expression that is different from the expression on the picture.

⇨ Sit next to the child and in front of the mirror. Make a facial expression in the mirror, and ask the child to make a different facial expression. Then ask the child to explain which features of the facial expression are different.

Making Faces

These exercises should emphasize to the students that not only must they be able to understand the facial expressions of others, but they also must be able to accurately communicate that expression to others.

For these exercises you will need a large drawn or cutout face and various facial parts (a selection of home-drawn or cutout pictures of eyes, eyebrows, mouths, etc.). Laminating the blank face and facial parts will extend the life of these tools.

⇨ Using pictures of high-intensity, medium-intensity, and finally low-intensity faces, ask the student to select appropriate eyebrows, eyes, etc. to create a similar and then different expressions on the blank face.

⇨ Ask your child to demonstrate a particular expression, and then photograph it with an instant or video camera. Examine the photos with the child, and discuss the accuracy of the expressions. For example, does the child's portrayal of a sad expression really look sad to the child? Encourage the child to focus on the way facial muscles feel when producing various expressions.

⇨ Describe various situations that children might encounter, and ask them to communicate appropriate emotions using only the face. For example, "Imagine that you are at the supermarket and need help finding a particular item. What facial expression should you use when asking for guidance? What sort of facial expression on others would indicate that they might be helpful to you?" Ask the children to create this face using the laminated pieces; once they have completed this task successfully, ask them to mimic the same expression with their own faces.

Varying Intensity of Expression

⇨ Establish whether or not your child is aware that people vary their intensity of facial expression to match a particular circumstance. For example, ask the child to sit in front of a mirror and show you the correct intensity of a happy expression for the following situations.
  • Your friend offers you some candy.
  • You get a good grade on a test at school.

- Mom and Dad buy you a computer, a bike, or some other surprise present.
Try this for the other primary emotions—sad, angry, and fearful—using appropriate examples.

⇨ Discuss with your child how the varied intensity of emotions often have alternative names attached to them. (Refer to the A to Z of Emotions on pages 180-181 for guidance.) Here are some examples:
- angry — exasperated, bitter, disgusted, enraged
- happy — contented, cheerful, delighted, ecstatic
- fearful — fretful, concerned, alarmed, terrified
- sad — upset, disappointed, miserable, gloomy, devastated

⇨ Using the A to Z of Emotions, draw up a list of low- to high-intensity emotions and see if your child can alter facial expressions accordingly. Discuss the appropriateness of using high- versus low-intensity facial expressions in various situations. A family member is more likely to compensate for an incorrect expression and respond accordingly than an acquaintance or stranger.

Varying the Angle of Expression

⇨ Explain to the child that facial expressions can look very different from various angles; as this is often all of the information people receive (especially in a crowded social situation), the ability to recognize an array of expressions from a 45-degree angle or side profile is a tremendously useful skill to possess.

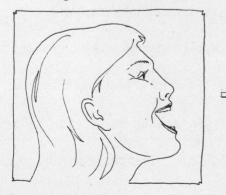

⇨ Use the three-way mirror to practice variation of angle expression. Begin by practicing emotions your child can express easily, especially happy, angry, sad, and fearful.

Ask the child to face the mirror wearing the appropriate expression for the emotion designated. Adjust the angle of the side wings so that one mirror gives the child a 45-degree-angle view and the other mirror provides a side-profile view.

⇨ Stand at an angle or in side profile to your child and make various facial expressions. See if the child can guess the emotion you are expressing. Begin with high-intensity expressions. Since both expressive and receptive skills should be practiced equally, trade places with your child so he or she can practice expressing appropriate expressions from a variety of positions.

⇨ Increase children's skills by talking to them about a particular topic or giving them an emotionally laden feeder line and see if they can produce the correct facial expression for that situation while listening to you. Move on to role-play situations, perhaps with a choice of "emotion," "angle," and "situation" cards.

Object Imaging

These object-imaging exercises focus the student's attention on detailed nonverbal information.

⇨ Provide photographs of complex situations (from magazines, newspapers, etc.) and present a pictorial situation to the child. Encourage the child to study any background information (buildings, scenery, etc.) which may prove helpful in deciphering the situation. Coach the child to study the picture for signs of movement (of people, vehicles, etc.) which might have a bearing on the scene.
  • Ask about the likelihood of sound at the scene. (For example, in a picture of a busy street or at a baseball game, the child would assess what sort of sound would be expected, then determine whether the sound would be friendly/pleasant or unfriendly/unpleasant.)
  • Ask the child to describe the mood of the picture. Is it happy, sad, angry, or fearful?
  • Ask the child to answer who? what? where? when? and why? questions about the scene.
  • Choose any character in the picture and ask the child to identify his or her nonverbal expressions.
  • Ask the child to concentrate, with eyes closed, on "seeing" the picture. While the child's eyes are still closed, ask the child to recall and to describe the emotions portrayed by the characters in the picture. Responses can be recorded for discussion if desired.

Once the child has mastered the photographic exercises, move on to the following exercises.

⇨ Watch videos of soap operas or movies with the sound turned off. Encourage the child to focus on the facial expressions of the characters and to attempt to follow the plot. Stop the tape at random, and ask the child to describe what is likely to happen next.

⇨ In public settings, such as shopping centers or athletic events, ask the child to observe people's faces from a distance and then try to guess the nature of their conversations and relationships. This can be turned into a game in which the child gets points for perceptions that agree with those of the tutor.

⇨ Play "face charades" in which only facial expressions may be used to provide clues to various emotional states or attitudes listed on cards chosen by the child. Have the child both "send" and "receive" these emotional states.

⇨ Play face lotto using the lotto base board on page 178. You can choose which nonverbal skills you want to match. For example, match facial expression to emotion, facial expression to gesture, or facial expression to paralanguage.

6

SPACE AND TOUCH

Most animals are territorial. They set boundaries around their dens or nests, and they will defend this space if necessary. Dogs often use odors to "mark" their territories (both outside and inside the house) so that other animals will stay away. Humans, however, usually define territory through ownership, delineating boundaries with tangible indicators like signs and fences.

T *ERRITORIAL SPACE refers to those places we feel attached to through ownership or identification.*

PERSONAL SPACE refers to a portable territory we all carry around with us.

USE OF SPACE

Territorial space refers to those places we feel attached to through ownership or identification. Most people are territorial about their homes, but neighborhoods, schools, and many other locations bring out a person's territorial instincts as well. Many gang confrontations focus on territory or "turf," and, on a larger scale, wars often begin over disputed land areas. When an individual walks into someone's yard uninvited or approaches someone's home, most owners become more alert and even tense because they feel their territorial space being violated. Sports like football, soccer, and basketball are territorial games based on defending or violating a specific space. Clearly, territorial space is an important concept in many aspects of our lives.

In relation to nonverbal language, our personal space is more important than our territorial space. Personal space refers to a portable territory we all carry around with us. As depicted in figure 6.1, personal space can be described as a flexible bubble that surrounds us. The bubble is wider in the back than in the front, and it contracts or expands depending on the situation. Children and adults who are socially successful are capable of understanding and utilizing space effectively in their interpersonal interactions.

figure 6.1
The personal space bubble

THE FOUR SPACE ZONES

It is amazing to realize how many space rules we must know and follow every day. As long as we follow these rules, people feel comfortable with us; as soon as we violate a simple rule of space usage, we risk the possibility of appearing weird or offending others. By the time we are adults, we are expected to know the necessary rules for managing personal space.

The diagram in figure 6.2 is based upon the research done by Edward T. Hall using American subjects. His research shows that inside the personal space bubble there are four zones within which it is appropriate for particular kinds of communication to take place. The first of these areas is called the *intimate zone*, which begins at nearly touching distance and extends out about eighteen inches. In this area, we permit close friends and family to relate to us and allow the discussion of intimate issues and feelings. Just beyond the intimate zone lies the *personal zone*, extending from about eighteen inches to four feet. We conduct conversations with friends and acquaintances in the majority of everyday settings in this zone. The *social zone*, which ranges from four to approximately twelve feet, falls outside the personal zone; it is appropriate to talk loudly in this zone so that people we have just met or are about to meet can hear us. Because there is a good chance that others can see what is taking place in the social zone, intimate, personal, and other private matters are not supposed to be discussed there. The final area, called the public zone, encompasses the largest amount of space, starting at twelve feet and ranging to infinity. We do not typically talk to people who are this far away from us; although we may see people who are in our public zone, we usually communicate with them through postures and gestures until they enter our social zone.

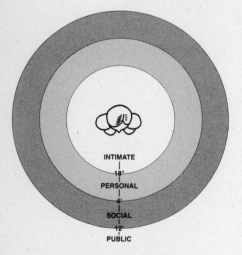

INTIMATE

18"

PERSONAL

4'

SOCIAL

12'

PUBLIC

figure 6.2:
The four space
zones

One of the most widely noticed nonverbal communication errors is the violation of personal space commonly known as "standing too close." Most of us know some people who do this; they make us uncomfortable and we tend to pull back and avoid them. These people are using the intimate zone for conversations that should take place in the personal zone.

Similarly, there are people who talk too loudly in the social zone about things that would be more properly discussed within the relative privacy of the intimate zone. For example, we knew a teenager whose mother frequently discussed family matters while in the social zone, thus allowing others to overhear and causing the youngster intense stress and discomfort.

Finally, moving further out into the public zone, there are people who, thirty feet or so away, will call out loudly, "Hi! How are you doing?" If you are like most people, you will react to this with some discomfort and will try to find some way to avoid answering until reaching the social zone distance of twelve feet.

Although children are given more leeway for space mistakes than adolescents and adults, they still can experience social rejection if they do not "obey the rules." We are indebted to the teachers with whom we have worked for giving us cogent examples of what one of them called "space invaders." Although very young children may frequently violate the personal space of others, they have to learn quickly where their space ends and others' space begins. For some children, learning this is difficult; if they drop something under the chair of a neighboring child, they are likely to reach down without saying the appropriate "excuse me," or "do you mind?" and thereby violate the other person's space—an action that may result in some kind of altercation. You may think that a child would know about the spatial zones intuitively, but this is not the case; spatial zones must often be taught directly. Demonstrating the need for overt instruction, one teacher describes a common space-invader encounter and her response:

"I was standing in the hallway speaking with the other second grade teacher when Jonathan came walking up the hall. We were in the middle of the hall, but there was room behind both of us for Jonathan to pass. As usual, Jonathan walked right between us and, as had now become my habit, I reached out and grabbed his arm gently and asked, 'What should you do if you see two people talking? How should you pass us? Between us or around us?' Jonathan, as usual, answered, 'Around you.' He retraced his steps back between us and then passed behind me. It took him a bit longer to learn this than most of his classmates."

Consider how verbal language affects personal space usage. Have you ever thought of why we must say "excuse me" in a polite voice when we enter another's personal space, especially the intimate zone? It is because we know that we are about to break a residual rule of personal space usage and are asking forgiveness in advance! If Jonathan learns to say "excuse me" in a polite voice when it is necessary to violate others' personal space, he will experience fewer of these sorts of problems.

Jonathan probably would have been served well by a technique that a very creative teacher described to us. She helped young children get a concrete sense of their own personal space by placing masking tape around their chairs and between children who shared tables. This made the personal space that some children already understood visible to everyone, and the all-too-common interpersonal problems caused by violations of personal space among her first graders all but disappeared.

Sometimes, space can be manipulated to increase the comfort level of the parties involved; often this involves moving closer to one another in order to foster trust or familiarity. One high school student involved in a tutoring program understood this concept completely and used his knowledge and intuition to help his younger students feel more comfortable.

James was part of a peer tutoring team at his high school. He and the other seventeen-year-old honor society students volunteered their time to tutor poor readers from lower grades. The teachers thought that fellow students would be less intimidating to the struggling readers than a teacher might be, and they assigned one tutor to each of the younger students.

The tables in the meeting room were arranged in two rows of five, with one chair positioned on either side of each table. When the tutors entered the room, they found the students already seated nervously, one to a table. All the tutors except James walked over and sat in the empty chairs exactly as they were positioned, that is, opposite the younger children. James, however, moved his chair to the long side of the table, near one edge; he also asked his student to move his chair to the narrow side of the table so that they were sitting much closer together. As the session progressed, this child appeared much more comfortable than the others.

When questioned about altering the seating arrangement, James explained his actions. He knew the younger child would be nervous, and he thought removing the barrier of the desk and reducing the "them and me" scenario would make the lesson much less threatening and confrontational to the child. The other tutors agreed that they must have appeared very businesslike and intimidating to the nervous students; in the next session, all of the tutors adopted James's sitting position. There were many more relaxed faces that day!

Cultural Differences and Space

While all people have a bubble of personal space surrounding them, the size and importance of the various zones change dramatically from culture to culture. When people of different cultures interact, they often have difficulties negotiating comfortable interpersonal space. It is important to be aware of the zones—intimate, personal, social, and public—of people from other cultures so that we do not inadvertently break a personal space rule when we are with them, or judge them harshly for different ideas of proper personal space conduct. For example, people from some Middle Eastern countries stand quite close during conversations. Americans in such a circumstance might feel like drawing back to a position that feels more comfortable to them. The Middle Easterners might interpret this as aloofness or disinterest.

MENTAL SPACE

Related to personal space is the concept of mental space. *Mental space* refers to the things we consider to be private, things like personal thoughts or topics of conversation which, if made public, might cause us embarrassment. It is important to explain this rather elusive idea to children in a simple but thorough manner. You may find this an opportune moment to talk about topics that we usually consider off-limits, especially in conversations with strangers. Some examples of taboo subjects are personal appearance ("Gee, your face is wrinkled."), finance ("How much does your dad get paid?"), and health ("I threw up last night."). Discuss which topics are appropriate in private places and which are appropriate in public domains. An adult may feel that a topic is clearly private, while a child may not feel that way at all; it might surprise you to discover the sorts of topics children consider suitable for general discussion. Parents must teach children the subtleties of discretion.

M*ENTAL SPACE refers to the things we consider to be private, things like personal thoughts or topics of conversation which, if made public, might cause us embarrassment.*

Once the child has a firm grasp of this concept, discuss warning signs that might indicate to children that they may have inadvertently invaded someone's mental space. The person might become flustered, stop talking, become agitated, get angry, storm away, cry, or simply state or imply that he or she is offended. Explain that it is appropriate to apologize immediately when you realize that you have broken a mental space rule. Also discuss helpful ways in which children can avoid having their mental space invaded. A statement like "I'm sorry, I can't answer such a personal question" can help to avoid conflict or discomfort.

USE OF TOUCH

How important is touch? Investigators Ronald Adler and Neil Towne think it may be the difference between life and death. Their studies revealed that during the nineteenth and twentieth centuries a large percentage of children died from a disease called "marasmus," which was directly related to the lack of human touch. Children in institutions such as orphanages and hospitals where personal contact was limited died regularly from this ailment. These children simply had not been touched enough, were incapable of healthy development, and died.

Human beings need more than just the biological essentials for life. We need to be touched and held in order to know we are loved. There are some who have even suggested that many Americans who suffer from touch deprivation turn to substitutes like drugs and alcohol to fill the void.

To understand the importance of touch, we must realize that it anchors one end of the personal space dimension; touching occurs at zero interpersonal distance. Having read what we have said about violations of residual rules, it should come as no surprise to you that anyone who touches us inappropriately, in terms of either the location or the intensity of that contact, stands an excellent chance of being viewed as strange or even frightening.

As an example of how intricate and refined the touching rules are, consider the following situation. You are standing behind someone who is involved in some activity. You do not know the person's name. How do you get his or her attention? Most people give the same answer: they would tap the person very lightly on the shoulder and say "excuse me." Most people know that the tap should be made very lightly on about a one-inch-square place on the shoulder equidistant from the neck and the end of the shoulder and that variance from this procedure will probably startle and frighten the person being tapped.

Why must we always touch people on the shoulder in this way? Quite simply, because *it is the accepted rule*! Why do we have to say "excuse me"? Because in order to touch someone, especially from behind, we have to violate that individual's personal space. Imagine your reaction if someone attempted to get your attention by touching you on the abdomen or the side of your neck. What if you were touched in the correct place on the shoulder, but with considerable force? In any of these situations your reaction would be negative.

There are many children who have not developed fully their sense of touch as a form of communication. Touch rules are especially hard to learn because they are so situational. The same child who understands and uses touch very well at home may need help in differentiating appropriate body contact behaviors at school or in other public situations. Usually these children are perfectly innocent in their intent, but other children and teachers can quickly respond in a negative fashion to behaviors that might be acceptable and even desirable at home.

A young boy we observed named Brad exhibited just this sort of confusion over public versus private touch. As we sat in the back of the auditorium during morning assembly, we saw several examples of Brad's problematic behavior.

Brad sat in the front row, one seat away from the teacher. Within thirty seconds of being seated he was hugging the child sitting next to him, and five seconds later the child was complaining to his teacher. The teacher told Brad to "keep his hands to himself," and Brad looked embarrassed. However, within another thirty seconds, he was resting his head against his teacher's shoulder; she responded by slowly but firmly pushing him to the upright position.

Many children like Brad are not aware that they are doing anything wrong; they are often puzzled and confused when things that they have always known to be positive, like hugging and snuggling, receive a negative response.

——————————————❑——————————————

The process of learning when, where, and how to touch others is a developmental one which requires patient and systematic teaching. Socially successful children learn quickly the rules of minimal touch that exist outside of American families. Perhaps it would be nice if the rules for touch were less rigid, but such is not the case. The best rule of thumb for most situations is "when in doubt, don't touch."

TOUCH RULES

Violation of touch rules almost always causes negative reactions. In an attempt to clarify touch rules, some researchers have conducted studies involving silhouette drawings of males and females, varying in age and identity. The subjects of the tests were asked where it would be acceptable to touch certain people; the silhouettes (an example is provided in figure 6.3) were described as being parents, siblings, girl and boy friends, and spouses. Most subjects agreed on where it is proper to touch and not to touch the silhouettes of different people. However, there were some subjects who did not seem to understand the proper vocabulary of touch and indicated they would touch areas of the body that most others would not. These subjects have problems with *expressive touch usage*—they don't know how to use the rules of touch.

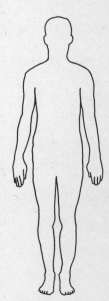

figure 6.3

Some errors of touching are more severe than others. The shoulder rule described on page 77 is one example. The touching of sexual areas, especially by someone who is above the age of eight, is considered an especially significant violation. In addition to these "taboo" areas for touching, there are also certain body parts that are to be touched only under certain circumstances. Research using the silhouettes we have described has shown that it is acceptable to touch others along the outside of their bodyline—that is, the outside of arms, the outside of legs, and so forth. In contrast to the relatively harmless touching that takes place on the outside of the bodyline, a touch on the inside of the bodyline is laden with emotion. When we touch a person in these places, we intensify the meaning of our gesture. These areas include the inside of our arms, the sides of our chest, and inside our legs and thighs. Misplaced or misunderstood touching can cause unfavorable responses.

In contrast to the relatively harmless touching that takes place on the outside of the bodyline, a touch on the inside of the bodyline is laden with emotion.

Clearly, differentiating between the inside and outside of the bodyline is important. If a teacher places his or her hand on the outside of a child's arm in a guiding position, the teacher suggests positive feelings about the student. When a teacher violates a child's inner bodyline by using a firm grip around the arm, the teacher sends a very different message—the student is in trouble. If this student is thinking, "Hey, I'm going to the principal's office to get some kind of an award!" he or she has a problem with receptive touch usage. When children don't know how to interpret others' use of touch, they are in for some big surprises!

Not only do socially successful children know *where* they may touch others, they also know *how* to touch them. There are many different kinds of touch, ranging from patting and squeezing to brushing and stroking. Each kind of touch communicates its own message. For example, we almost always use a pat to communicate something positive. In contrast, a squeeze can be either positive or negative depending on the circumstance. The poke, however, is almost always negative, but is especially negative when used on sensitive areas of the body.

The upper chest area is such an area. When most people in the United States refer to themselves, they point or touch their upper chest area (often near or around the heart). If you direct an anger-provoking touch—like a poke—at the spot which represents the essence of the other person, you can be almost sure of a confrontation. Would a similar reaction follow the poking of someone's forearm? Probably not.

If children have difficulty with either expressive or receptive touch skills, the best way to begin teaching them proper touch etiquette is to talk about touch. Discuss the messages children send when they touch other people. If you find that they have problems expressing the correct intensity of touch, make them aware of the difference by giving examples of inappropriate intensity of touch. If a young child hits a dog instead of patting it, the dog will respond negatively, and the child will probably feel confused; the child thinks he or she is sending a positive message, yet the dog replies with a negative message. Help children practice variation in their touching intensities and locations. Remember, young children are seldom aware of the variation in intensity of touch and may need additional assistance.

Cultural Differences and Touch

As with personal space usage, there are extensive cultural differences regarding rules of touch. According to studies of different cultures, we in the United States are among the least prone to touch or be touched. In fact, of all the countries of the world, only the British seem to prefer less touching than we do. Most Americans are probably quite content to keep their personal space bubble relatively large and to have that space violated as seldom as possible.

An interesting study of contrasting cultural touch behaviors was conducted by Sidney Jourard. He observed the number of touches per hour that took place between couples in cafés in four different locations: Gainesville, Florida; London, England; Paris, France; and San Juan, Puerto Rico. Consistent with other studies concerning cultural differences in touch, couples in the United States averaged only two contacts compared to 180 and 110 touches for couples in Puerto Rico and France, respectively. Only the English couples touched less than those in the United States; in fact, they didn't touch at all.

Even though Americans frequently prefer not to touch or be touched (or perhaps because of this), touch plays a significant role in our relationships.

Even though Americans frequently prefer not to touch or be touched (or perhaps *because* of this), touch plays a significant role in our relationships. The teacher who knows how to rest a soft hand on the shoulder of a student who needs encouragement, the parent who gives a supportive hug to a child to encourage or reward a job well done, or the child who gives a teammate a properly intense "slap on the back" during a game are all effectively "speaking" nonverbal language. On the other hand, children who misuse touch are likely to have interpersonal relationships that are fraught with tension, difficulty, and all too often, social rejection.

SPACE AND TOUCH

USE OF SPACE

Laying the Groundwork

Learning the rules and the variations of appropriate space usage is a complex task. The following exercises train children to understand and use space effectively when relating to other people.

⇨   Begin by asking children to explain what they understand by the word "space."

⇨   To develop an awareness of space variation, ask children to observe people sitting on park benches or sofas or standing in line for lunch; point out that, unless there is a good reason to do so, they are not touching each other. Have older students keep a diary for a few days describing how much space people seem to need or allow in various situations.

⇨   Help students make a list of public places where awareness of personal space is important. Examples could include parks, libraries, swimming pools, public transport, churches, and restaurants. For each location, list the ways people protect or delineate personal space. (Lanes in a swimming pool, family names on pews in church, and reservation cards on tables in restaurants all serve this purpose.) Discuss appropriate and inappropriate personal distances for each location. While more than one person can swim in a pool lane, the swimmers must be careful to say on the proper side of the lane, neither hampering the lane swimmer nor any other swimmers.

⇨   Make a poster to illustrate the results of your discussion.

Estimating Distances

⇨   Working one-on-one, allow the child to establish a comfortable and appropriate distance from you. Then shift your position either closer or further away and ask the child to readjust as well. Do this several times, role-playing in different situations (at the park, at a mall, at home).

⇨   Give children a large piece of paper and ask them to draw how long they think a centimeter, an inch, or a foot is. Ask them to use their hands to show you how long eighteen inches and then two feet would be. Periodically check with a measuring stick to see how accurate they are. In a large room tape a fifteen-foot length of rolled paper to the floor (or use a rug at home). Ask children to step off distances of eighteen inches, four feet, and twelve feet, marking each spot with masking tape. Once again check their accuracy with a measuring tape and make a tape mark at the correct distances. (Remove the incorrect markings.)

If children have difficulty with the tape markings, use familiar everyday objects for reference to help them judge distances. For example, "an arm's length" or "the distance from one end of the sofa to the other," etc.

Recognizing and Maintaining Proper Distances

⇨ Introduce the ideas of *intimate*, *personal*, *social*, and *public space*, and make sure the child has a solid understanding of the words.

⇨ Mark these words and distances on your floor plan.
  • intimate = 0 inches to 18 inches
  • personal = 18 inches to 4 feet
  • social = 4 feet to 12 feet
  • public = 12 feet to infinity

⇨ Set out a six-foot strip of masking tape on the floor. Have your child stand at one end of it while you describe an imaginary person standing at the other end. Ask the child to walk toward the "other" person, stopping in an appropriate zone. Include among the "imaginary" people parents, siblings, teachers, police officers, principals, friends, enemies, strangers, and the like. This exercise will reinforce an awareness of the need for spatial variations, while teaching children to observe and use appropriate distances themselves.

⇨ Create some relationship cards—mother, father, sister, brother, teacher, clergyman, stranger, friend, etc.—and ask children to place them at an appropriate distance from themselves for a conversation.

⇨ Ask children to stand at the zero mark on the six-foot strip of tape. Adopt a role from one of the relationship cards used in the previous exercise and act out your approach. Help the child to "read" the situation effectively. Is this a friendly, safe situation or should the child be careful? Is this person someone who wants to play with the child or not? Some examples to try: a stranger stopping very close to the child and a peer stopping far away.

Practicing Comfortable Interpersonal Distances

⇨ Reproduce the Comfortable Interpersonal Distance Scale on page 72, and, using the same relationship and role-play cards, test your child's understanding of the use of spatial zones.

⇨ Make a large chart with your child to show who would be permitted into each of these zones, adding a discussion of the tone of voice required and the type of conversation you might hold in each. Make this table bright and colorful and keep it as a permanent record of the session. Put it up in the kitchen, bedroom, or classroom. Encourage children to ask questions about it.

You may wish to color code the table so that green denotes people and conversations which are allowed in this zone and red signifies people and conversations which are definitely not allowed in this zone. Remember to include such exceptions as nurses and doctors.

⇨ Talk about how people allow their personal space bubble to alter in size depending on the situation. Make a list of comparable public and private activities and talk to the child about how the location of the activity affects the child's space bubble. For instance, a child's personal space bubble would expand if he or she were talking to a stranger, but in the presence of a parent, the personal space bubble would become smaller. In general, we allow those we know well closer to us than those we do not know well. A child's personal space bubble will expand in most public situations.

This exercise should increase the child's understanding that private situations are usually the most secure, while public situations require that we leave more space between people.

Learning to Use Personal Space Without Conflict

⇨ Engage children in hypothetical conversations with various characters to check if they thoroughly understand the use and the many unwritten rules of spatial zones. Use this opportunity to raise awareness about situations which you as a parent feel are particularly important, such as a stranger offering your child a candy bar. If the child has been taught correctly, a stranger walking into his or her personal zone should immediately set off alarm bells. These conversations can serve as a lead-in to a discussion of signals that indicate an invasion of personal space. Ask children how they would feel if someone invaded their personal space—uncomfortable? angry? scared?—then explain that this is what others feel when you unthinkingly invade their personal space.

⇨ Ask children to remember occasions when their space was invaded and when they invaded someone else's space. Help children understand the emotional consequences of misusing personal space.

⇨ Compile a warning list of possible conflict situations where personal space is either restricted or shared. Examples might include group work at school (shared tables), art lessons, locker rooms, bedrooms shared with siblings at home, and the family living room.

If children are aware of the possibilities of conflict, they should become more conscientious in minding the personal space of others. Help them see that when space is restricted or must be shared, *organization* and *negotiation* are the golden rules to avoiding conflict.

⇨ Discuss, negotiate, or role-play who is and who is not allowed in certain territorial space locations. Should the mailman come inside the house? Should a brother be allowed in the child's bedroom? Use this exercise as a guide for negotiating ground rules for your personal household or classroom.

⇨ Discuss the idea of "private topic" areas, then help children make a list or picture diagram of these areas.

⇨ Prepare a "Rules of Space" reminder poster listing appropriate topics for discussion with people of different degrees of acquaintance and in differing situations.

USE OF TOUCH

Laying the Groundwork

⇨ Begin by asking children to define what they understand by "touch."

⇨ Ask the child to help you make a list of the emotions we can convey through touch. For example:
- anger, aggression, disapproval, fury
- alarm, fright, guilt, surprise, distress, shock
- sympathy, sadness, calm, grief, hurt
- sappiness, love, affection, caring, kindness
- apology, gratitude, praise

Then ask the child to convey each of these emotions to you by means of a touch. At this stage *where* they choose to touch is not as important as *how* they touch. This exercise will highlight any types of touch with which the child has real difficulty. Record names for each touch the child gives you, such as punch, slap, pat, etc.

⇨ Ask the child to compile a list of different types of touch, to divide the types into two categories, "positive" and "negative," and to describe what they convey. The types of touch should be ranked high-intensity, moderate-intensity, or low-intensity for each category.

See if the child can identify how the intensity of a certain type of touch can alter meaning, as well as how using the incorrect intensity can convey a completely different emotion to the receiver. A pat on the back given too forcefully may feel like an angry shove. A parent might rest a hand lightly on a child's shoulder to convey approval of what the child is saying; the same parent, however, could send the opposite message by pressing a finger firmly into the same shoulder.

Learning the Art of Touching

⇨ Discuss the factors we must consider before we can touch someone appropriately, such as our relationship to the person and the length of time we have known the person.

⇨ To demonstrate the complexities of close contact, touch children in various places, varying the places of touching (inside bodyline versus outside bodyline) and the intensity of the touch (for example, a pat versus a push). Ask them what is communicated by each touch.

⇨ Collect pictures or make cards depicting different categories of people, such as friends, a shopkeeper, waiter, aunt, or brother. Role-play situations using the cards and ask the child to suggest appropriate touch to convey a particular emotion. For example, to express thanks to a good friend, a smile and a hug would be appropriate; to a new friend, just a smile; to a shopkeeper, a smile and a handshake; to an aunt, a kiss.

⇨ Make a game of thinking up extreme incongruities like kissing a shopkeeper, shaking your mother's hand, or hugging a delivery man. Expand the game to include a discussion of the various space zones and the types of touching that are appropriate in each. What kinds of touch would be allowed in the personal space zone but not in the public zone? Who should children allow to touch them intimately? socially? publicly?

⇨ Observe others touching each other in natural settings and during common interactions (at school, at the mall, in church, at home). Discuss the ways in which touch communicates things between the people involved. Help children understand that they can learn a lot about the way others feel by watching their touching behavior. For example, based upon how a teacher is touching another child, should you or should you not do what that child has just done?

⇨ Through use of a touch silhouette, such as the one in figure 6.3 on page 79, focus on the areas of the body that one may touch. Be sure to explain the different touch behaviors associated with various situations and people. For example, have your child indicate the places where it is okay to touch Dad versus a teacher, Mom at home versus Mom at the mall, etc.

⇨ By tracing around a figure in a magazine or catalog, make four silhouettes: a female adult, a male adult, a female child and a male child. Ask children to choose a character from a list you have prepared. This list might include the following:
- parent
- child
- doctor
- teacher
- brother
- sister
- friend
- girlfriend

Then ask them to select an appropriate silhouette for that character. Give them a situation, such as comforting an upset character. Ask children to point to the area where they would touch them. It is best to have them verbalize the spot to avoid confusion. Ask them to indicate the intensity of touch they would use. Any errors should be discussed in detail with each child. The explanations will have a more lasting effect if you arouse an emotional response from the child. It is up to you as the parent or teacher to decide how involved you want to get; if there are subtle messages that you wish to convey to children concerning touch, then this is the ideal opportunity to do so.

⇨ Encourage children to learn the subtleties of appropriate touches for private and public settings. Make a short list of private and public places, like home versus school or grandmother's house versus a restaurant. Negotiate with your child to determine what you both consider an appropriate touch in these places. You may find that while children love to receive a big kiss at home, they feel acute embarrassment if you give a similar kiss in front of their classmates!

7

GESTURES AND POSTURES

We don't need to be very close to people to learn a great deal from their nonverbal patterns. Although most of us pay little attention to our own accompaniments to verbal language, we tend almost unconsciously to ascribe great import to the gestures of others. Gestures and postures are long-distance communicators, revealing details about ethnic origins, level of energy, attitude, and motivation. People who use them well appear in a very positive interpersonal light.

THE COMPLEXITY OF GESTURES

From the simple learning of how to "wave bye-bye" to the more complex learning of intricate finger and hand positions which express an array of emotions, gestures play an increasingly important role in our moment-to-moment interactions. Children who can interpret other people's gestures—as well as produce a broad repertoire of clear and understandable gestures themselves—hold a distinct advantage in interpersonal relationships.

Since we use an array of gestures, from very blatant to quite subtle, in daily interactions, it is impossible to list them all. Still, being aware of the sheer number and complexity of our gestures helps us communicate better. This awareness is hard to attain because most of the time, gestures occur as background to the conversation and do not stand out.

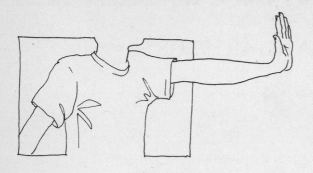

figure 7.1

For our most important gestures we use our hands to convey a wide variety of information. Sometimes arms, hands, and fingers are used to produce *batons* which emphasize, complement, or specify the meanings of words. For example, when you want to communicate "Stop," an assortment of gestures can accompany the word to achieve effects of differing intensity. When someone is coming toward you, you could put your hand out. To halt a commotion, you might wave your hand at waist level in front of your body. If the word "Stop" is accompanied by the hand motion in 7.1, the meaning is much stronger than it would be without the hand motion. Of course, there is always the word "Stop" accompanied by the finger-pointing gesture in 7.2. This baton typically says, "I mean business," and frequently is used when teachers or parents are disciplining children.

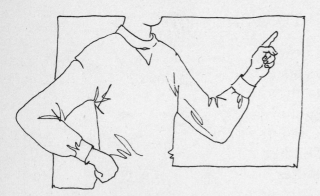

figure 7.2

Some gestures embellish words, while others can communicate information independently of words. In most areas of the world, a shake of the head means "no" and a nod of the head means "yes." Similarly, crossing the arms tightly in front of the chest most often communicates resistance, sticking out the tongue communicates defiance, and tapping or shaking the foot communicates nervousness or impatience.

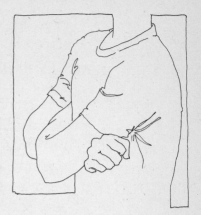

We have examined, with the sound turned off, videotapes of children who are highly successful interpersonally. This procedure magnified the gestural behaviors of the children, moving information that is typically in the background to the foreground. Most of these children used their hands to communicate in very effective ways. Their gestures were synchronized with their other gestures or with their postures, and were clear, positive, and easy to follow. Richard was one such child we observed.

Richard was the natural choice for captain of the school rugby team. He was always present to lend support through both good times and bad, and his skill in using expressive gestures made him a leader. If the team was doing well, he ran around them with infectious enthusiasm, cheering and waving his arms, giving thumbs-up signs to the spectators, slapping the players on the back, and giving them high fives. When times were tough and the team was going through a bad spell, he could lift the spirit of the entire group with encouraging and commiserating gestures such as a shrug, a slap on the back, or a supportive arm around the shoulder. Every member of the team felt valued and cared for under Richard's leadership, and his intense but appropriate gestural displays of emotion improved the team's performance and helped establish a large following of similarly motivated fans.

Children need to know which gestures to use and when they are appropriate, knowledge Richard clearly possesses. Richard's nonverbal language is geared specifically towards a group and an athletic competition; slaps on the back or high fives, highly effective on the playing field, would be out of place and ineffective in a formal setting like a classroom.

Gestures add immensely to our ability both to send and to receive complete information about feelings. Further, in interpersonal relationships, gestures often provide the basis for the "true" meaning of a conversation. Therefore, if we want to maximize the effectiveness of our gestural communication, we must make sure that our words and gestures match. Consider, for example, one child saying to another, "Get away from me!" If the words are accompanied by a gesture meaning dislike, such as a raised fist, the message of rejection is clear. However, if that gesture were to accompany the words, "Let's go," the meaning would become confused; the words would be paired with a gesture of opposite meaning. As mentioned before, research shows that when verbal and nonverbal messages are at odds, the listener is more likely to believe the nonverbal one. This last point is crucial. If children are unaware of their gestures, it will be difficult for them to interact with people. Other people assume that our gestures match our internal states; therefore, what they see is what they respond to.

The more aware we are of how gestures affect our interpersonal interactions, the better the chance that our interactions will be positive. Children who use appropriate gestures and are aware that they are using gestures effectively are more likely to be socially adept.

THE POWER OF POSTURE

As compared to gestures, which usually involve specific body parts, *postures* involve most or all of our body, including a combination of torso position, hand and arm location, foot location, and head orientation. Although a posture consists of many components, we typically respond to each posture as a

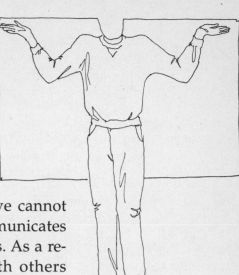

single unit of nonverbal behavior, a "message" that tells others about such things as our general mood, our degree of commitment to an activity, our basic attitudes, or our level of self-awareness. Because postures use so much of an individual's body, we can often "read" postures from far away as well as up close.

While it is possible to avoid making any gestures or touching other people, we cannot avoid showing a body posture that communicates something about our attitudes and feelings. As a result, we are always communicating with others through our posture whether we mean to or not. Teachers claim that they often can judge a class on the first day of school by looking around at the ways in which the students are sitting. In a similar manner, parents often can tell the kind of day their children will have by the way they sit at the breakfast table. Most children do not go around "pos-

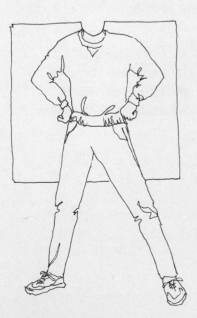

turing" in an active or calculated way. In fact, most youngsters (as well as adults) pay little attention to how they are holding themselves as they sit, stand, or walk. If children increase their postural awareness and learn to use postural communication effectively, they can improve their chances for social and academic success; if they don't, they may experience significant, unintentionally induced problems.

RESTING POSTURE AND IMAGE

Postures communicate a great deal to others, and our lack of attention to them can be the source of "mysterious" social success or failure. We have found that most people have a comfortable posture that they assume when they are not feeling or doing anything particularly special. This "resting posture" is probably the posture most often seen by others. If a child slouches badly when seated, leaning forward with back bent and head down, we see this child as disinterested, or even as incapable. Conversely, if children are seated upright with heads and eyes forward, they appear to be "ready for action" and open to new experiences and interactions.

When Karen began sixth grade, she was an extremely witty, highly intelligent young lady. Unfortunately, her resting posture of folded arms and her low-pitched, loud, gravelly voice made her appear aggressive and hostile. She was the black sheep in the high-flying academic set because she did not possess the finer social skills of her peers.

At first her classmates and teachers saw her behavior as an idiosyncrasy and a source of amusement. However, by ninth grade their feelings had changed. Other students teased or rejected Karen, and many teachers formed negative opinions of her.

Karen knew that she did not fit in with her classmates, and therefore decided that she wasn't as bright as others academically either. The net result was a downward spiral of decreasing effort and declining self-esteem. She took on the role of the class rebel and did badly in examinations as a survival mechanism that expressed all the stored-up hurt inside her.

"Resting" postures are not the only body positions that communicate relationship information. Let's consider the average school classroom, a place where body postures play a very important role. Imagine a good teacher at work who uses body postures expressively in a very effective manner. One such teacher we observed learned to use her desk for different postural positions depending upon the importance of the lesson at hand. When the topic was a loose and lively one, she stood, legs crossed, leaning back on the front of her desk. For a more serious topic, she stood firmly on her two feet at the side of her desk. For the most serious topics, she stood behind her desk, leaning forward, with her hands resting on the desktop. Most of the children  could adequately understand postural language and would respond appropriately according to her changes in posture. However, in several of her classes she noticed a few children who did not alter their behaviors in response to her postures. These children were either not aware that she was assuming different positions or, if they were aware, did not realize that these different postural positions had any specific meanings. All children need to learn about the importance of their own posture as well as that of others so that they can adapt to the ever-changing social situations around them. Such adaptation is related to social and academic success.

Lucy and Laura both ranked in the upper academic echelon in high school. They were best friends and sat next to each other in class. Both girls obtained similar grades

for classwork and homework assignments, yet while Lucy was perceived as an interested and attentive scholar, Laura was viewed as being disinterested and poorly motivated. Typical comments on Lucy's report card read "Always gives her best." On the other hand, Laura's comments typically included statements such as "Laura keeps much of her ability in reserve," or "Could try harder."

Why was there such a difference in opinion as to how much effort these two girls put into their studies? Much of it had to do with their postures. Lucy always sat upright in class and faced the teacher. She looked ready to learn, as if she were absorbing the teacher's every word and enjoying the experience. When she moved about from class to class, she carried herself very well and projected a positive image. Laura's posture was very different from Lucy's. Laura slumped in her seat or sat with one leg curled up beneath her; she often put her head on the desk while the teacher was talking. Therefore, even though she may have been listening just as well as Lucy, she appeared slovenly, slow, uncaring, or bored. Teachers did not feel that she particularly wanted to be there. In general, she projected a negative image. Something as simple as posture helped to account for Lucy's success and Laura's perceived weakness.

WALKING

Up to this point, our discussion has focused on relatively static postures—that is, postures that are used by people when they are basically remaining in one spot. However, when people move themselves from place to place, they also engage in a sequence of postural changes which can communicate information. What we are describing is a "gait," or a way of walking. Impressionists sometimes find that copying a celebrity's distinctive way of walking is the easiest way to capture that person's personality. Two classic examples of a person whose walk served as a "signature" are John Wayne and Groucho Marx.

Every day we notice and interpret the information that walking transmits, from the shaky gait of an elderly person to the threatening swagger of a "tough guy." People form initial long-distance impressions of others based upon their walking style; for example, we are more likely to attempt to start a conversation with someone who has a friendly walking style than with someone who has a menacing, street-tough walking style.

Gaits not only affect our relationships, but also our adjustments to unfamiliar settings. People raised in small towns must learn that the streets of a large city call for completely different behaviors than they may be used to. While smiling at passersby and strolling at a slow, leisurely pace are common in smaller towns, such behavior on the busy streets of New York City would be highly unusual. Indeed, especially for women, such behavior can even lead to an increased chance of harassment. Most people living in cities walk rapidly, keeping eyes down and avoiding eye contact. In other words, "city" street posture and gait project a no-nonsense attitude and do not invite contact between people. If we do not wish to be seen as weak on a potentially dangerous city street, we should stand and move with confidence so that others will perceive us as strong and competent.

GESTURES AND POSTURES

GESTURES

Laying the Groundwork

⇨ Begin by asking children what they understand by the word "gesture." Ask them if they know various common gestures. For example, does your child recognize that thumbs-up equals "okay" and that a finger over the mouth means "be quiet"?

⇨ Work with your students to generate an A to Z "picture-dictionary" of gestures using newspaper or magazine cutouts, photographs, etc. Help them organize this dictionary and use it for specific nonverbal language tasks such as nonverbal charades (in much the same way as children use verbal-language dictionaries).

⇨ Using their personal A to Z of Gestures along with the A to Z of Gestures at the end of this book, ask children what emotions they think are expressed by various common gestures. Select emotions that you feel are the most important for each individual child. Ask children to give an appropriate gesture for the emotion that is presented. Keep a checklist of the gestures they already know and of the gestures they feel unsure about; this will highlight areas of difficulty.

⇨ Discuss the difference between positive and negative gestures and have children classify the gestures in the A to Z list as either positive or negative. Children can mark the gestures represented in their gesture dictionary as positive or negative by adding a "P" or an "N," or by color coding.

Using Gesture to Convey Feelings

⇨ Make a set of cards labeled with those body parts commonly used in gestures.
- hands
- fingers
- shoulders
- arms

Make a set of "message and emotion" cards, including items such as:
- frightened
- "Hello!"
- "Be quiet."
- "Look!"
- bored
- "Come here!"

Select appropriate combinations of "message and emotion" and "body part" cards and ask your child to attempt to convey the message or emotion using that body part. To illustrate how often hands are used in gestures, have the child use only the head and arms to show various emotions or messages.

⇨ Set up games or other activities in which children may only use gestures or other nonverbal patterns to communicate. We highly recommend charades, a powerful nonverbal tool.

To play charades, prepare three types of cards: feeling cards (anger, boredom, etc.), method cards (space, facial expression, gestures, etc.), and send/receive cards. Fifteen cards for each category should be sufficient. (A spinner on a circular chart can also be used if desired.) Have a child pick one card from the send/receive pile. When the card says "send," the child picks one card to determine which feeling is to be expressed and another to decide the method by which to send it. The child then acts out the feeling while the others try to guess what it is. When a child selects a "receive" card, he or she chooses another child to be the sender. The sender draws a feeling card and a method card; the receiver then tries to guess the feeling the sender is acting out.

"Reading" Gestures

⇨ Tape and watch television shows or movies in which people often exaggerate gestures for effect. (Slapstick comedy shows are one good choice.) Discuss with the child the relationships between the characters involved. Demonstrate and discuss the relationship between gestures and the characters' emotional states and how one can use this information to interpret the situation. For example, point out the gestures of one character, stop the tape, and talk about what is likely to happen next.

⇨ Encourage children to become aware of background gestures in television programs or movies. Have them keep a record of the number of positive compared to the number of negative gestures in favorite programs. (If the child doesn't like the words "positive" and "negative," substitute "pleasant" or "unpleasant.")

⇨ Watch mimes perform (library programs and videos are good sources for material) and discuss what they are "saying." Do not assume that all children understand these artists; it is surprising how many children are simply lost when watching them.

⇨ Make videotapes of your child in routine activities such as playing outside, sitting at a work table, waiting in line, having lunch, etc. Sit down together and watch the tapes without the sound, identifying positive and negative gestures. Discuss the situational appropriateness of gestures.

⇨ Increase your child's understanding of nonverbal gestures by discussing situations in which certain gestures would not be appropriate. Gestures appropriate in private situations may not be acceptable in public situations. For example, while in an emergency pointing might be considered appropriate, during a religious service it is considered rude.

Provide a humorous example of an inappropriate gesture in a public situation for the child to use as a reference. Being sent to the principal's office and tapping your foot impatiently when he arrives late is a good example.

⇨ Play gesture-word lotto, using the playing board on page 178. Make nine cards that name specific gestural messages. Then write the same gestural messages on another nine cards, placing one in each square of the lotto board, face up.

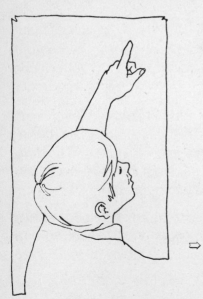

Make the gesture indicated on one of your cards. Ask the child to choose the matching verbal card on the board. If the choice is correct, the child turns that card face down. When the child has flipped all of the cards on the board, the game is over. For example: The adult chooses a card that says "Stop!" That adult then tries to express that message to the child through gesture. If the child correctly identifies the gestural message, he or she may flip the matching card on the lotto board and proceed to the next gestural message until all the cards on the board have been flipped over.

⇨ For an individual or class activity, have a child stand behind a screen or sheet with a source of backlighting. Ask the child to draw a card with a gesture pictured on it or a card with a word on it implying a gesture. Have the child perform the gesture, which is projected as a silhouette onto the screen. The parent or class audience then tries to guess the meaning of the gesture.

⇨ Develop a cross-cultural program for studying gestures. Obtain magazines (such as *National Geographic, Stern, Elle,* etc.) or television shows from other countries, and identify differences in gestures and their meanings. (See the "References" section for suggested readings; a good one is *Bodily Communication* by Michael Argyle.) Help children understand that different cultures communicate the same message with different gestures. For example, saying hello can be expressed by a handshake in North America and Europe, by a kiss in France, and by rubbing noses in the South Sea Islands.

⇨ Give your child examples of good and bad gestural manners.

GOOD MANNERS
- smiling when meeting a new classmate
- talking quietly in a library

BAD MANNERS
- pointing at people

POSTURES

Laying the Groundwork

⇨ Begin by asking children the meaning of the word "posture." If they do not know, help them to see that the position of our bodies is "read" by others as an indication of our mood or attitude. One good way to assess children's abilities to "read" postures is to show them videotapes without sound (as described earlier in our discussion of gestures). Watching videos without sound makes it easier to focus on a wide variety of postures in adults and children who are interacting under different emotional conditions.

Help children understand that we do not always adopt a posture which corresponds to our true feelings. Emphasize that representing feelings with posture is important; if other people think we are feeling something that we are not, it can cause miscommunication.

⇨ Make an A to Z "dictionary" of postures using magazine pictures or personal photos. Label the postures according to their meanings, such as "tired," "bored," "angry," etc.

⇨ Using the A to Z of Postures on pages 180-181, explain to students that

postures can indicate either positive or negative emotions. Together, classify each emotion in the A to Z as positive or negative either by adding a "P" or an "N" to the end of the word or by highlighting positive and negative emotions in different colors. If you prefer, help children create a new list under the headings "positive emotions conveyed by postures" and "negative emotions conveyed by postures."

⇨ Ask children to stand in front of a mirror and show you an appropriate posture for each emotion. As they demonstrate postures, record some of the positions they choose for use in further exercises. If possible, collect pictures or photographs of the postures. List different words commonly used to convey similar emotions beside each appropriate posture. For example, "angry" and "annoyed" could be placed together with the same posture.

⇨ To further convey that we attach meaning to postures, ask your child to walk with a variety of gaits. How would a soldier walk? An elderly person? A cowboy?

Resting Posture

⇨ Explain "resting posture" to children and discuss why resting posture is important. Be sure that children understand that it is not what they *feel inside* that people respond to, but to how they *look on the outside*. If a child's posture says, "I'm bored," people will believe this message even if the child protests that he or she is interested in what others have to say.

⇨ Determine children's resting posture in both standing and sitting positions. (If possible, have them sit or stand in front of a full-length mirror.) Does their posture convey a positive or negative emotion? If positive, which parts of the posture are positive? If negative, which parts of the posture are negative?

⇨ Discuss resting positions and ask children what kind of resting position they are likely to adopt. For example, what postures would they have in the following situations?

AT HOME
- watching TV
- doing homework

AT SCHOOL
- sitting at desk
- standing talking to teacher

⇨ Together determine whether resting postures at home and at school should differ. Discuss the merits of having a positive resting posture, such as appearing more friendly, interested, and approachable to others.

⇨ Incorporate humor. Ask students how appropriate it would be to go for a meeting in the principal's office and lie down on the couch, or sit upright with legs together and both feet on the floor while watching a movie and eating popcorn at home.

Learning to Create Postures

⇨ Play "feeling" charades (refer to the directions on page 99), using postures as the prime method of nonverbal communication. Be sure your child has a chance both to give clues (expressive communication) and to receive them (receptive communication).

⇨ Play posture lotto. Using the lotto base board on page 178, write down a selection of emotions (one in each square). Give children a picture corresponding to the emotions and ask them to place the picture on the appropriate squares until the board is completely covered.

⇨ Provide practice in "long distance" communication. Have children observe various people and then describe, purely on the basis of posture, the internal feelings, attitudes, and characteristics being communicated. Encourage them to think about the implications of various postures seen from a distance. Does posture help them to decide whether to approach or avoid people?

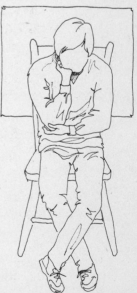

8

RHYTHM AND TIME

Rhythm is probably the most basic type of nonverbal communication and is present earlier than most other forms of nonverbal language. An intriguing experiment emphasizes this point. Metronomes set to sound at different rates of speed were placed next to newborn infants and the amount of time it took the infants to fall asleep at different speeds were recorded. It was found that infants fell asleep quickest when the metronome was set to correspond to the heart rate of the infant's mother. It appears that children in infancy have already learned to discriminate among rhythms and to favor one, similar to the mother's heart rate, above others.

Rhythm is not only important in its own right but plays a part in most other parts of nonverbal language. For example, the speed and tempo of verbal speech has emotional impact above and beyond words that are spoken. As children mature, they learn the rhythms of the people around them and the rhythm of their culture as a whole. With awareness of our own and others' rhythms, we can choose how we apply our rhythms and other qualities of time, especially as adults. We can also dramatically influence others' attitudes about our personalities, especially in relation to our reliability and commitment. Once individuals become aware of the messages they are sending with their rhythms and their use of time, they can take steps to improve both expressive and receptive time usage skills.

DEFINING RHYTHM

One of the authors of this book grew up in Wisconsin and another in New Jersey. For years, the Wisconsinite felt rushed by the Jerseyite, while the Jerseyite was frustrated by what he saw as the Midwesterner's slow, methodical approach to just about everything. When we would attend conferences in the Midwest, one of us always felt "right at home," while the other was uneasy. However, the situation was reversed when we attended professional meetings in New York. There, one was comfortable with the chaotic and hectic pace, while the other was made anxious by it. Over the years, we learned to adapt to each other's rhythms and reach a comfortable interpersonal compromise. Two people who want to establish a relationship must learn to adapt to each other's rhythms.

As shown by our personal example, rhythm has both receptive and expressive components. *Receptive rhythm* usage refers to the ability to recognize the rhythms of others and to know what those rhythms mean. *Expressive rhythm* usage refers to an individual's ability to adjust personal rhythms to harmonize with others and to express specific feelings or attitudes. The ability to synchronize personal rhythms to fit those of other people puts them at ease immediately and decreases the possibility of misunderstandings and discomfort.

Because few adults and children are aware of this most subtle of all nonverbal language forms, almost all children can benefit from practice in this

RECEPTIVE RHYTHM usage refers to the ability to recognize the rhythms of others and to know what those rhythms mean.

EXPRESSIVE RHYTHM usage refers to an individual's ability to adjust personal rhythms to harmonize with others and to express specific feelings or attitudes.

area. Several of the tips presented later in this section are aimed at nurturing these abilities.

RHYTHMIC DIFFERENCES AND COMPATIBILITIES

Rhythmic differences and compatibilities play an important part in interpersonal relationships. Being "out of sync" with others can make children feel anxious and uncomfortable. When a person's rhythm is too fast, it may make others feel rushed, uncomfortable, and nervous. If a person's rhythm is too slow, it may make others feel impatient, annoyed, or even angry. A very slow rhythm can also give others the impression of ignorance or apathy.

We observed one child whose difference in rhythm caused a great deal of friction within his family unit.

Nick was the second of three children; his older brother and younger sister were the biological children of his parents, but Nick had been adopted when he was a baby. His siblings did well academically and socially, but Nick seemed to be troubled. As we observed his family in its daily functioning, we saw that Nick was "out of sync." At the dinner table, while his parents and siblings ate quickly, Nick ate very slowly. In fact, he did almost everything at a slower pace. Inevitably, the family would become impatient and annoyed with him.

Nick's emotional rhythm also differed from the rest of his family. While his family was quite emotional and reacted strongly to situations, Nick's reactions were moderate. His parents often misinterpreted this different level of responsiveness as an indication that he did not care about things that they cared about. Although he tried as hard as he could, Nick could not match his rhythm to theirs; among the results were all-too-frequent misunderstandings and parent-child conflicts.

When Nick's parents became aware of the rhythmic differences at work in their family, they also became much more tolerant of Nick's behavior. With some remediation, Nick also recognized his rhythmic patterns and tried to shift his behavior accordingly. The family ultimately began to work together to synchronize their rhythms, and thus eased the family's internal conflict.

Fortunately, people *can* learn to accurately "read" and then synchronize their own rhythms to those of others. Pat, a very effective elementary school teacher, had the ability to make other people feel at ease around her, though they rarely could say why. When we observed Pat on a playground with a number of her students, we began to understand that her ability to make others comfortable was due in large part to her skillful use of rhythm. When Pat was with a child who walked or ran rapidly, she matched that child's pace; when with a slower child, she slowed down. Pat made children comfortable by matching her rhythm to theirs. Regardless of the child's gender, social or ethnic background, or daily mood, she communicated her understanding of that child through her nonverbal behavior.

NATURAL RHYTHMS

In addition to keeping in mind personal and cultural rhythms in the way Pat did, it is also important to become aware of children's natural rhythms. Many parents report that changes in rhythm strongly affect their youngsters. If children are used to getting nine hours of sleep and only get seven, if they get up late or miss breakfast, or if they have to get up an hour earlier because of daylight savings time, their rhythms may be adversely affected, thus making children less interpersonally adept. While most children will adjust to rhythm changes after a few days, an awareness of these shifts can often help parents and teachers to understand and minimize potential problems.

Another way parents and teachers can apply their knowledge of rhythm is to plan tough activities for times when they and the children are at their best. Most teachers know that difficult subjects should be taught at the times of day when children are at their sharpest, just as many parents recognize shifts in their child's attention span. Utilizing this knowledge is a simple but important way to recognize and take advantage of personal and natural rhythms.

THE USE OF TIME

Expressive time usage describes the behavior by which we say something to others through the use of time. We can tell others that they are very important to us by spending time with them or by waiting for them if they are delayed. To say that our friends and family are important to us means little if we do not spend a significant portion of our available time with them. Thus, giving of our time is one way we communicate caring.

We also can demonstrate respect for others by the use of time. Punctuality definitely has a communicative value. How many of us have repeatedly been kept waiting by someone and have perceived that person to be uncaring, self-centered, and irresponsible? Most people see the ability to be on time as both a responsibility and a desirable quality. In a related sense, the time we are willing to wait for someone can be directly related to the status of the person involved. For example, anyone who has ever been to a busy physician's office learns what waiting for a high-status person is all about.

Time management is also an important aspect of expressive time usage. The ability to estimate time requirements for duties

> **G**iving of our time is one way we communicate caring.

and events, to sequence time effectively, and to schedule time accordingly all fall into the category of time management. One student we observed had developed a personalized and highly effective time-management program that clearly helped her academic career.

Lisa kept impeccable time. She was always one of the first to arrive at class regardless of the location of her last lesson; she always completed work assignments in the time allocated, never too early as some had a tendency to do, but never late; and her homework was always beautifully presented, unrushed, and meticulously researched.

Lisa's secret was a diary, which she had kept from the sixth grade. In it she recorded the contents of each lesson and details of homework assignments, due dates, and sometimes the amount of time that it had taken her to complete a task. As she was a member of several school organizations, she also recorded lunchtime and evening meetings in her diary.

Because she had such a good idea of how long a particular teacher's homework would take, she was able to distribute her homework tasks evenly throughout the week. This also allowed her to enjoy a full social calendar outside of school. Some children who engaged in very few extracurricular activities often complained of having insufficient time to devote to homework, or would forget to attend a scheduled meeting, but Lisa, who had such a hectic schedule, never once had to make excuses for herself. Several of Lisa's friends regarded this meticulous recording as unnecessary, yet she was the first and last resource for any child who needed to know an assignment's due date.

Because she was so time conscious, Lisa never kept anyone waiting and could always be relied upon to turn up for important events; she was highly regarded by teachers and peers alike as a mature, responsible, and conscientious individual.

By the eleventh grade, Lisa's concept of time was so internalized that, when she took standardized tests like the SAT, she had no problem proportioning the allocated exam time to allow herself a fair chance of giving each answer her best effort. Consequently, she never fell into a trap like many of her peers who, not having learned the importance and value of good time management, spent too long on earlier questions and then ran out of time in later sections.

CULTURAL DIFFERENCES

Significant misunderstandings can develop if time cues are misread or misexpressed. For instance, if you are invited to a party that is scheduled from 7:00 P.M. until 9:00 P.M., when should you arrive? According to Judee Burgoon and Thomas Saine, two researchers in nonverbal language, it depends on which part of the country you are from. If you are in New York or Chicago, arriving anytime from 8:00 P.M. on is acceptable, but not right at 7:00 P.M. However, if you are in Salt Lake City or a small town in the South, you should arrive as close to 7:00 P.M. as possible without being early. In one instance, arriving on time would be rude; in the other, arriving late would be inexcusable. Clearly, the communicative use of time can be a powerful factor in social success.

As with all nonverbal communication, culture plays an important part in the communicative meaning of time. Just as rhythm varies in different regions of the United States, the meaning of time varies from culture to culture; it is important to recognize this in order to prevent miscommunication. In American culture, sayings such as "time is money," and "Why put off 'til tomorrow what you can do today?" are common.

There is a reason why fast food establishments got their start in the United States. However, we must realize that not all cultures and people share the view that lunch is something to finish as quickly as possible. Many cultures consider the mid-day meal the primarily meal, spending several hours eating and socializing before returning to the workday world. For example, many French schoolchildren go home at noon to share the largest meal of the day with their families, while most American schoolchildren hurry through cafeteria or brown bag lunches, usually eating the largest meal of the day at home in the evening.

RECEPTIVE TIME USAGE

The flip side of the expressive use of time is receptive time usage. *Receptive time usage* involves understanding the way others use time to communicate to us, and it is just as important for social success as sending appropriate messages to others through our use of time. Sensitivity to the meaning of time factors is a very subtle skill, but it is a skill that people must master to be socially successful. When people are aware that social and academic interactions take place in time, they can use this awareness to help them achieve their interpersonal goals.

> RECEPTIVE TIME USAGE involves understanding the way others use time to communicate to us.

Time cues are an important source of interpersonal information. For example, a child must learn that if a teacher says a homework assignment requires two hours to complete, it should not be glossed over in a few minutes; it is "serious" homework. Similarly, if a child is told to be in the principal's office at 10:00 A.M., the child should realize that even if the principal has not appeared by 10:10, the child should continue waiting.

One of the most crucial features of time usage, at least in

the United States, is the ability to be on time. This is a skill that requires a great deal of practice, but it is especially important in our culture. People who consider punctuality a bother and are notoriously late for things often provoke resentment and frustration in those around them. Therefore, they may be rejected or avoided, and they simply may not know why. Developing the skills to read and express time information accurately can often spell the difference between success and failure in a relationship, be it personal or professional.

PRIVATE VERSUS PUBLIC TIME

One final aspect of time deserves some note. Many children do not understand the difference between private and public time. *Private time* is time to be alone with one's thoughts, time to work things out, to organize, and to dream. Our concentration is usually better during private time, so this is a good time to think or study. Explain to the child that everyone needs private time, and that interruptions during these periods can be especially annoying to others. *Public time* is time to share experiences and to communicate with others; this will probably be an easier concept for your child to grasp. School and family outings are two examples of public time.

Because they seem so obvious and insignificant, we can easily overlook rhythm and the use of time as forms of communication. However, our experience has repeatedly shown us that these components of nonverbal language can have dramatic impacts, both good and bad, on our well-being. Parents and teachers who help children to develop skills in these areas are helping to build a foundation upon which interpersonal success may later rest.

PRIVATE TIME *is time to be alone with one's thoughts, time to work things out, to organize, and to dream.*

PUBLIC TIME *is time to share experiences and to communicate with others.*

RHYTHM AND TIME

Rhythm

Laying the Groundwork

⇨ Begin by discussing with children what they understand by the word "rhythm." Help them see that a rhythm has a regular beat, and explain that things that have good rhythm are in harmony. Use images of situations without proper rhythm, like an orchestra without a conductor or flying trapeze artists that are out of sync, to help children understand this concept.

⇨ Have your child observe the rates of various behaviors in others and try to parallel those rates. For example, ask him or her to clap with you as you vary your rate of clapping, or swing at the same pace as another child on a swingset.

⇨ Ask children what things in their everyday life have a rhythm. These examples can include a clock or watch, music, heartbeats, and athletes in tennis or hurdles. Make use of each of these examples to distinguish between rhythms which can, and those which cannot, alter their speed.

⇨ Discuss the fact that no one can alter the rhythm of a clock. A second always lasts a second. A minute always contains sixty seconds. The speed in which time passes does not change.

⇨ In contrast to the unchanging rhythm of a clock, a heartbeat is an effective example of changing rhythm. Many children believe that their heart beats at a constant rate. Have them count their heartbeats over six seconds and multiply by ten to get their heart rate. Then ask them to jog in place or perform some other exercise. Ask them to calculate their heart rate again.

⇨ Children may never have noticed the bassline or the beat in their favorite songs, but they will be able to tell you that songs can be "fast" or "slow." Play an example of some slow music. Have them clap out the beat. Next play an example of a faster song and ask them to clap out the beat. (If the children already play musical instruments, they will already have a fairly good understanding of rhythm.)

⇨ Tape yourself talking. Count the number of words you use in a minute. Then make a tape of the child discussing rhythm with you. Play the tape for one minute and count the child's words to determine the speech rate. When you compare the two, generally you will find that the child speaks faster than the adult. Ask the child to tell you who is speaking faster; if he or she cannot differentiate between the rates of speech, the child may have difficulty "reading" rhythms.

⇨ If you have a metronome (or a Newton's Cradle), show the child how to talk at the rate of the metronome. Alter the rate and hold a conversation with the child at that rate. Discuss how artificial this is, and make the child aware that we need some variety in our rate of speaking. Help children listen for other people's talking speeds, noting that some will talk faster than the children and others will talk more slowly.

⇨ Have the child practice speaking, playing, or writing at different speeds. Ask him or her to read some sentences that have strong emotional meaning at different rates and to think about how the rates of speech change the effect of the sentence. Here are some sample sentences:
- "Hey John! Look out for the tree!"
- "I'm so sorry you lost your cat."
- "Don't you ever take anything from my room without asking again!"
- "Wow, this is just what I wanted for my birthday!"

⇨ Discuss and show children how the rhythm of speech contributes to the meaning of sentences. Let them tell you why a certain sentence should be said at a certain speed. For example, in the case of a dangerous situation, a fast rhythm is appropriate because of the need to inform others quickly.

⇨ Just as it is important to adjust the rhythm of our speech to particular situations, it is also important to adapt our bodily rhythm to certain activities. Use a video recording of an athletics event or an actual visit to one to show a child how important correct use of rhythm can be. The three phases of the triple jump or the measured number of strides between hurdles provide perfect examples of the importance of rhythm. Ask the child what would happen if the athlete loses the rhythm. The runner might fall over, collide with hurdles, and ultimately lose the contest. (This is an image which tends to stick.)

Rhythm and Emotions

⇨ Use photos or cutouts from magazines that depict situations in which it would be appropriate to slow or increase the speed of behavior. For example, look for scenes showing people trying to catch a train or plane when time is short, or waiting in a long line to get into a movie theater. Describe other situations in which changing the speed of behavior might be necessary and ask children to role-play such situations.

⇨ After practicing some of these exercises, children should be able to suggest the appropriate rhythm for individuals expressing any of the emotions listed below. Ask children what their own rhythm should be when responding to such an emotion.

IF AN INDIVIDUAL IS	THEIR RHYTHM IS	THE APPROPRIATE RESPONSE IS
• happy or excited	• fast	• fast
• sad	• slow	• slow
• angry	• fast	• slow—to calm situation
		• fast—to escape danger
• fearful	• fast	• slow—to calm person
		• fast—to escape danger

⇨ Ask children when and where it might be important to adapt their rhythm. Ask the child for examples in the home, in public places, and at school where a fast or a slow rhythm might be appropriate.

As a parent or teacher you can use these discussions to approach problem areas such as arrival at class, work rate, getting ready in the morning, etc. Here are a few examples:

HOME

FAST RHYTHM
- tidying up for visitors
- getting ready for school

SLOW RHYTHM
- entertaining visitors
- carefully completing homework
- dressing for a special occasion

PUBLIC PLACES

FAST RHYTHM
- exiting a burning building
- fleeing from danger

SLOW RHYTHM
- walking in a crowded mall
- walking in church

SCHOOL

FAST RHYTHM
- working to finish a timed lesson
- returning from recess

SLOW RHYTHM
- moving from class to class
- speaking before an audience

Keeping a Record

⇨ We recommend that you keep a record of your discussions about rhythm. The form of the record should be appropriate for the age of the child.

For a young child, the record might be a brightly colored card on which the child or the parent could draw symbols to represent particular situations. Older children could be asked to create a table or chart like the one on page 115, perhaps using color to indicate a fast or slow rhythm (green for fast and red for slow). The child's chart could also include cultural rhythms showing how people from differing backgrounds vary rhythmically. For example, your child could compare the stereotypical "slow" pattern of talking in the American South and the quick, staccato pattern of speech in the Northeast.

TIME

Laying the Groundwork

⇨ Begin these exercises by discussing the child's definitions of "time," "time usage," "estimate," and "punctuality." As a fun way of starting the discussion, ask children (or the family or the students in your classroom) to think of as many expressions involving the word "time" as they can. For example, phrases such as "in the nick of time," "a stitch in time saves nine," and "time flies when you're having fun" can be used; titles of books, songs, or movies are also good starters for this game.

Time Management

⇨ Practice time estimation with children by asking them to estimate the passage of various amounts of time. For example, ask them to tell you when thirty seconds or one minute has passed, then correct them and practice timing as needed.

⇨ Find out if children can tell you at what times and in what order they do routine things in an average day. Many errors concerning time usage occur because of an inability to sequence events. Provide a list of activities your child does on an average day and ask the child to write down the time each activity occurs.

WHAT TIME DOES THE CHILD

• get up?	• have morning recess?	• arrive home?
• eat breakfast?	• eat lunch?	• eat dinner?
• begin school?	• finish school?	• go to bed?

Ask the child to estimate the time it takes to accomplish these everyday activities; this will highlight the child's ability to judge time. For example:

HOW LONG DOES IT TAKE THE CHILD TO
- get dressed?
- eat breakfast?
- walk to the bus stop?
- ride to school?
- eat lunch?
- get home from school?
- do homework?
- eat dinner?
- watch television?
- get ready for bed?

Record these estimations on a chart. Do not comment at this stage as to whether the child is correct or incorrect with these estimations.

⇨ Then ask children how long they would *like* to spend doing each of the activities above, record these comments on the chart, and add up the hours. It is most likely that the child overestimated the number of hours in a day or left insufficient time for sleep. If your child has underestimated time, this exercise is just as important; underestimation can lead to chronic lateness. In either case, use the results of this exercise to show that time management is important because it allows us to "fit in" a combination of things we both want and have to do each day (such as work and leisure activities).

⇨ Over several days, help your child record the actual time it takes to do each activity. You may have to time younger children, while older children can use a clock or a stopwatch to time the activities themselves. Add the actual times to the estimated and desired time chart. Post this chart where the child can refer to the results when trying to manage his or her time.

SAMPLE CHART

ACTIVITY	TIME ESTIMATED	TIME DESIRED	ACTUAL TIME
• getting dressed	• 30 minutes	• 10 minutes	• 40 minutes
• brushing teeth	• 5 minutes	• 1 minute	• 2 minutes
• doing homework	• 1 hour	• 15 minutes	• 3 hours

Compare the child's estimates with the actual time records. The areas the child grossly overestimated or underestimated are problem areas; focus special attention on these areas on the posted chart to keep the child aware of them. For example, if you see from the chart that children have consistently overestimated the amount of time spent on school chores (that is, they think they spend an hour on homework when in fact they only spend half an hour), then you may want to devise ways to help them learn to judge time duration. A timer or stop-watch are useful for this purpose.

⇨ Describe several situations that involve judging time duration. Include both good and bad scenarios. Discuss the consequences of being a good timekeeper versus a bad one. Use an actual, recent incident and talk about how it might have come out differently if time had been estimated differently. For example, you might say, "Remember the night you stayed up until twelve o'clock reading the materials for your book report? Would you have done anything differently if you knew exactly how long it takes you to read thirty pages?"

⇨ Teach ways of estimating accurate "travel" times. Describe some places that children must go and provide a target time for their arrival, for example, walking to school and arriving at 8:00 A.M.. Ask them not only to tell you how long it should take to get to the destination, but also what time they need to start the journey in order to arrive on time.

If the child has difficulties, provide some tips such as overestimating to arrive a bit early. Use a progress chart to keep track of and illuminate the child's improvement.

⇨ Provide an inexpensive watch that has a built-in stopwatch. Teach children how to set the watch for a "time for task" or "time for travel" estimation. Demonstrate how the watch can then be used to guide the speed of working, walking, etc.

Punctuality

⇨ Ask questions about punctuality issues like honoring time commitments and the emotions that promptness and tardiness might invoke in others. If you are late, what does that mean to a friend who is waiting for you? How is this different from keeping a teacher waiting? A school principal? A physician? A grandparent? How do you feel when you are kept waiting by various kinds of people?

⇨ Have children keep track of the number of times they are late for something and how often they are on time or even early. Ask them to chart their progress as they try to improve from week to week.

⇨ Make a list of situations when it is important to be on time. You might include:
  • leaving the house for school in the morning
  • arriving at lessons
  • meeting someone like Dad, a coach, or a friend
  • arriving home after playing outside

⇨ Make a list of the characteristics we associate with being late and early.

LATE
- lazy
- irresponsible
- disrespectful
- uncaring

EARLY
- responsible
- respectful
- caring
- loving

⇨ Ask children to think of examples of times when they were late. Get them to describe the occasions and then think about how people reacted and why they reacted in that way. Ask what the other people involved must have thought. What should we do when we are late to make sure people don't get the wrong impression? (Apologize and give an explanation at the earliest opportunity.) Explain that people will generally accept lateness from time to time, but not if it is a regular occurrence.

Public and Private Time

⇨ Discuss the difference between personal time (private) and public time (shared). Make sure your child understands the difference.

⇨ Discuss the advantages of private time with your child. Private time can be quiet, relaxing, and completely personal. Explain that with no private time, a person would likely get restless, be disorganized, have no time to think, and no time to calm down after an argument.

⇨ Ask your child to describe the effect of having no public time. Some examples include loneliness, isolation, and the inability to learn (most of our learning comes from interacting with the world around us). This exercise should teach children to respect their own time. Then move on to discuss the public and private time needs of other people, such as mother, father, siblings, teachers, and friends.

⇨ Make a sheet listing private times for family members. For example:
- brothers/sisters/self doing homework after dinner
- Dad doing paperwork at home
- Mom getting ready to go to work or out for the evening
- teacher marking papers

If desirable, involve the whole family and post the sheet in a public place as a reminder.

9

OBJECTICS

Most people are only faintly aware of the nonverbal behavior patterns discussed so far—patterns dealing with the location, position, and movement of the body, as well as the use of voice. Because they are less aware of these channels of communication, they typically do not try to control them. In this chapter, the focus shifts to a different channel of nonverbal language called *objectics*. This channel deals with things that many of us try to control—the ways we communicate to others through our *appearance,* such as our style of dress. In contrast to other kinds of nonverbal communication, objectics often reflect *rapidly changing* aspects of our culture. Whereas a particular gesture or facial expression may remain the same from generation to generation, when it comes to style and appearance, what is "in" and what is "out" can change very quickly. Proper communication through appearance can be maintained only when a person is in tune with his or her culture's changing sense of fashion. This factor makes objectics a very complex area of nonverbal language, both expressively and receptively.

In contrast to other kinds of nonverbal communication, OBJECTICS often reflect rapidly changing aspects of our culture.

Objectic signals include cosmetics, clothing, jewelry, hairstyles, perfumes, and deodorants. The cars that we drive, the kind of furniture in our homes, and the foods that we eat also fall into the realm of objectics. These elements are important in communicating who we are, but because they go beyond those things that are "attached" to us directly and because they are usually associated with the adult world, we will not discuss them further here.

Two concepts very important to the discussion of objectics in children, however, are image and impression. *Image* is an idea that exists both within a person's mind and in others' eyes. People carry around images of themselves at all times; they think of themselves as competent, confused, overweight, beautiful, old—any assortment of emotionally laden concepts. People also unconsciously project their self-images onto those around them, affecting the way others react to them. An individual may try to project different images in different situations—a businesslike image at work, a less formal, more friendly image during personal time, or an intellectual image at school. Clothing and other objectic signals can dramatically affect the image a person presents to others. An *impression* differs from image in that it exists only in others' eyes; it is a receptive quality only. Therefore, you can make a good (or bad) first impression on someone else, but you cannot "express" an impression—it is completely external from you. Thus, no one can be completely sure about the impression he or she makes on others. The impression people make on others is also dramatically influenced by objectics. While these concepts may be elusive to younger children, it is important to explain them to your child. Be sure to teach children that their objectics send signals

I MAGE *is an idea that exists both within a person's mind and in others' eyes. People carry around images of themselves at all times; they think of themselves as competent, confused, overweight, beautiful, old—any assortment of emotionally laden concepts.*

An IMPRESSION *differs from image in that it exists only in others' eyes; it is a receptive quality only.*

to others, projecting an image and influencing others' impressions. Also discuss that their self-concept, as expressed through their objectics, has direct implications for the impression made on others.

STYLE OF DRESS

Style of dress communicates that individuals wish to be seen as part of a group; conforming to style helps them avoid standing out as strange or different. For example, most young adolescents tend to follow somewhat rigid rules of fashion. In fact, the particular jeans your teenager "must have" may be just as important for school as your professional outfit is for the office. The people in each respective group are sending the messages: "I am a safe, predictable person to be around," "I am like you," and "You can trust me."

Style of dress is the one type of nonverbal language that has inspired efforts to specify formal rules to guide it. We are referring to dress codes for schools, restaurants, and other social settings ("No Shoes, No Shirt, No Service"). One successful attempt to tell people how to dress was developed by John Malloy, whose books for aspiring business professionals on how to "dress for success" became bestsellers. Just walk down Madison Avenue in New York at noon and you will see that many of his rules for business dressing are still being followed.

> *Style of dress is the one type of nonverbal language that has inspired efforts to specify formal rules to guide it.*

EXPRESSIVE OBJECTICS

While style of dress most often reflects a desire to "fit in," objectics can also be used to communicate individuality, inner feelings, or personal attitudes. If it accurately reflects inner feelings and attitudes, then a person's style can be an effective way of attracting potential new friends. A skillful use of objectics underlays the immense interpersonal success enjoyed by Helen, a delightful youngster from Newcastle, England.

Every teenager "forced" to wear a school uniform goes through a stage of attempting to individualize it. Helen was no exception, but she altered her uniform in such a way that hers actually looked better than the original! When most girls were shortening their skirt hems, Helen lowered hers. When oversize sweaters and shirts were "in," Helen wore fitted blouses and cardigans. Yet she never looked overdressed or "older" than her sixteen years. When dyeing and teasing hair was popular, Helen's hair remained its natural brown and was neatly pinned up; she also never cluttered her face with makeup. One by one others began to copy her because she gave the impression of being in control of her life.

Outside of school, however, Helen appeared quite differently. She wore the latest fashions, let her hair down, and wore makeup just like her peers, although she still had an edge—an eye for color and the ability to make unusual combinations of clothing work. She was still the girl that everyone wanted to look like.

Helen's secret was that she knew how she wanted to be treated and the image she wanted to convey, both in and out of school. She used her appearance and dress—the language of objectics—to send those messages to the important people in her life… and it worked.

Most parents know how important it can be for children to have "the right clothes" for school and social events. In our modern society, sport shoes and clothing have come to be so important, for example, that some children have been beaten—

even killed—by others who covet their "special" objectics. Parents and children alike are often pressed financially in an effort to dress stylishly. But all children aren't able to have the things they want. In many families, younger children must wear "hand-me-downs" or clothing that is ill-fitting or out of style. While most adults empathize with these situations, children are often less able and sometimes less willing to accept people who dress unstylishly. Like it or not, the concept of a "nerd," "geek," or "loser" is all too frequently intimately connected to clothes and how they are worn.

Creative parents can be very resourceful. Clothing that is "in style" need not be outrageously expensive. Some parents find relatively easy-to-make patterns for stylish clothing in magazines or fabric stores. Others shop carefully in a wide range of discount stores for "designer" clothing. Some parents have even improved their children's wardrobes by taking imaginative looks at the clothing in their own closets and adapting items to the current teen styles. We have seen teachers set up dressing, hairstyle, and personal hygiene groups in schools where children can learn to maximize their resources in a club-like atmosphere.

> Focusing solely on the negative can have markedly destructive effects, especially in young adolescents.

Having a limited income is not the only obstacle to dressing well. Some children (and some adults) don't have a clear sense of how their appearance impresses others. They may not be aware of the potential negative connotations of wearing their pants too high or too low or of wearing out-of-style clothes. Such children are usually unaware of how their appearance affects others, and it is difficult to say anything to them for fear of appearing rude or hurting their feelings. However, when teachers and parents offer feedback in a sensitive manner, most of these individuals are eager to improve their dressing patterns. As a child begins to progress and dress more appropriately, positive feedback can be even more effective. A simple, "You really look nice today," can go a long way in helping a child to recognize the power of his or her style. Focusing solely on the negative can have markedly destructive effects, especially in young adolescents.

Yet fashion is actually a very small part of objectics. Clothes that are too trendy can be less appropriate in some situations than out-of-date clothes; we want to focus on dressing well, with a sense of self and with an image in mind, rather than dressing in up-to-the-minute fads or ultra-fashionable outfits. We certainly are not advocating conformity of dress either; we want children to understand objectics as a group of elements that affect the way other people react to them and to take responsibility for the image they project to others.

BODY SHAPE AND FORM

In addition to makeup, hairstyle, and other objectic patterns we have described, the shape and form of one's body has also become an important channel for nonverbal communication. In recent years, great emphasis has been placed on how people maintain themselves physically. The growing number of runners, walkers, swimmers, body builders, and other amateur athletes in America testifies not only to a new health consciousness but also to the importance our society places on looking fit, slim, and agile. Most of us would like attractive and well-conditioned bodies that would send to others the message that we are in good shape. Because of this, body development can be used to help children who are socially apprehensive or hesitant. Consider what happened to Hassan, a slightly built eleven-year-old who disliked attending school.

Every day, Hassan wept quietly on the school bus; his tears would not stop until 9:00 or 9:30 A.M., after which he seemed to be all right for the rest of the day. Hassan had few friends, and was the butt of many jokes and much ridicule because of his uncontrollable crying.

After observing him for several months, the school's PE teacher recommended to Hassan and his parents that he begin a personalized weight-training program. That teacher knew that research had shown weight training and noncompetitive running or swimming to be excellent self-esteem builders because practicing these sports almost always guaranteed improvement. With the help of a friendly weight-training instructor at the local health club, Hassan slowly began to train and strengthen his body. One year later, Hassan had become a different child. Here was a smiling and confident boy wearing a T-shirt which showed off his new physique. He reported that he was no longer afraid to go to school and that many of the other boys were friendlier to him.

When he felt better about his physical appearance, Hassan's fear of school disappeared, and he no longer communicated vulnerability and fear. His expressive objectic communication was much improved, as were his social and academic experiences.

RECEPTIVE OBJECTICS

As we continue to consider communication through objectics, we need to focus on its use as a receptive language as well as an expressive one. For example, receptive accuracy in "reading" style of dress can be an extremely important tool, not only in establishing social relationships but also in maintaining a child's safety. We spend a great deal of our time as parents teaching our children about whom to approach and whom to avoid. One of the first things we teach them is that when they are in trouble, they should find a police officer. How are they supposed to identify a police officer? By being able to read the "meaning" expressed through a police uniform.

There are many other situations in which understanding style of dress in others is equally important. If a child is lost and a police officer is unavailable, what sorts of people should the child seek out? Strangers with satanic tattoos on their arms and safety pins through their noses? A man dressed in a business suit? If a child is looking for someone to play baseball with, should he ask a child dressed in a football uniform?

BODY ODOR, HYGIENE, AND YOUR CHILD

While clothing can be a difficult thing to talk about with children, an even knottier issue is body odor. It is almost impossible to ignore children whose personal hygiene habits are so poor that they smell bad. In America, we have come to expect others to have clean hair, sweet breath, and fresh-smelling skin. (Americans seem obsessed with extreme cleanliness when compared to other cultures with more relaxed standards of hygiene.) We often see these elements of hygiene as basic to social interactions at home, in the workplace, at play, and in school.

We tend to avoid people who do not practice good hygiene. Adults are usually polite in such circumstances and will rarely, if ever, mention the problem. As we noted when we talked about clothing, children are not always so polite. Often they will mock children with unattractive body odors, calling them hurtful names. The result is painful to think about and to watch.

While the outward signs of body odor can often be "fixed" after thoughtful discussion and guidance, the heart of the problem is a little more complicated. *Children who have hygiene problems are usually unaware of the expressive power of their poor personal hygiene;* they are simply oblivious to the reasons behind any avoidance or teasing. For this reason, children need to learn about the signals body odor sends to other people, as well as effective hygiene techniques to avoid body odor.

Often children do not understand the concept of hygiene as an activity, nor do they know how frequently they should perform particular hygienic activities. If you see a need, discuss those activities you wish to include in your child's regular hygienic routine in a nonconfrontational manner; also discuss how often each item should be done. Include activities such as washing hair, washing face and hands, bathing, changing underwear, and brushing teeth. For older children, also include topics like using deodorant, shaving, and removing makeup.

OBJECTICS

Laying the Groundwork

Objectics may be the most difficult nonverbal channel to discuss, especially with children who are particularly sensitive or with children in certain age groups. The activities that follow are designed with these difficulties in mind.

⇨ Explain the concept of "objectics." Make a chart of words that fall into this category, including hygiene, style, image, and dress. Discuss these words and make sure the child understands them.

Add a section to the chart for attractive and unattractive qualities, and ask children to name things under each heading that they think makes a person attractive or unattractive. They may bring up such items as makeup, jewelry, hairstyle, and clothing. For example, under hygiene a child might name clean, shiny hair or dirty fingernails. Ask them who they think spends more time on their appearance and who thinks more of themselves, attractive or unattractive people? Encourage them to talk about how they perceive the way we look as affecting how we feel and how others feel about us.

Projecting an Image

⇨ Ask your children if they believe it matters how they dress. Hopefully they will answer "yes." Move on to discuss a person's image and arrive at a personal definition for the word. Make it clear that image and fashion are not the same thing.

⇨ Discuss with children the difference between a positive and a negative image. Ask for examples of people with a positive or a negative image.

⇨ Make a list of many types of people and ask the child what the standard image is for each one.
  • nun: black-and-white habit, simple hairstyle, pure look
  • construction worker: muscular, tanned, wearing a hard hat, jeans, and sturdy boots, often a man
  • gang member: tough, wearing certain gang colors, young male or female

⇨ Ask what clothes the people listed would wear and why they are important. Try to lead children to figure out for themselves what impressions people can make with clothes alone.

⇨ To emphasize that image and fashion are different, dig out some old photographs of you or your parents looking rebellious, casual, etc. Children may laugh at the outdated fashions, but they will probably get the point. The fashions they wear today will seem out of style and even odd in a few years. Explaining this concept to a teenager can ease conflict situations over appearance between parents and teenagers.

⇨ Define guidelines for a dress code with your child. Use the discussion about impressions and image to help. Ask the child what impression they would like to make. Be sure to modify the dress code for specific locations; an outfit acceptable for school might not be appropriate for the synagogue.

⇨ Move on to incorporate fashion in the discussion of image. Talk about how certain items of fashion are more or less appropriate in certain situations and how they add or detract from the image we wish to create. For example, no matter how in fashion hightop sneakers are, you probably wouldn't wear them with a party dress. Dressing conventionally in certain situations avoids distracting from the image you may want to project.

⇨ Watch television or examine magazines with children and then complete the following exercises together.
  • Discuss how styles of dress reveal personalities or feelings.
  • Discuss inappropriate matches of professions or activities and dress. For example: Would it be appropriate to jog in an evening dress? Would a doctor look professional wearing a football helmet?
  • Ask what feelings the child would have about a person dressed inappropriately.

⇨ Buy or make a paper doll and cut outfits for it from a clothing catalog.
  • Name a particular situation or location, and ask the child to dress the doll appropriately.
  • Give the doll a profession and let the child dress the doll for particular situations or locations.
  • Dress the doll yourself and give the doll an identity. Ask the child if the doll is dressed appropriately and what impression the clothing portrays. Include some ridiculous mismatches for fun and to emphasize how inappropriate people can look.

⇨ Go to a mall and visit different kinds of shops with your child. Watch people dressed in various ways and take turns trying to guess which stores they might go into or would not go into. Develop this into a game with points and other rewards for accurate "reading" of style-of-dress cues. Discuss the ways that clothing can give us clues to other people's personalities, interests, attitudes, and values. Is someone dressed unconventionally (wearing leather pants, with a pierced lip and dyed purple hair) likely to enter a shop specializing in men's business suits?

⇨ Collect pictures of children and adults in a variety of clothes. Ask children to guess the personalities, interests, or attitudes of the people in the pictures from their clothing. When they are finished, show them a list of your own answers for comparison. Make comparing answers into a game so that you can discuss any discrepancies in a relatively stress-free manner.

⇨ Create age-appropriate situations that require children to seek help from others.
  • Provide pictures of people dressed in different styles and discuss which individuals would be appropriate to approach and why.
  • Get children to describe the "uniform" worn by particular people in society. For example: a policeman, a doctor, and a rock star.
  • Focus on why each individual dresses as they do, then discuss the essential parts of their uniform. (Being able to recognize a person as a member of a particular profession can be very useful, especially in emergency situations.)

⇨ Provide a variety of different types of clothes, makeup, jewelry, perfumes, deodorants, colognes, and other fashion accessories. "Assign" children a personality or attitude to portray and allow them to select an outfit. Have children explain why they have chosen certain items to depict their assigned personality.

Fashion

Because fashion changes so rapidly, parents and teachers should not trust their own instincts or memories regarding what is acceptable. Instead, adults should observe children in school, at the shopping mall, on television shows, and in magazines in order to establish a child's-eye view of the currently acceptable trends. Do not believe the old adage, "If this style was good enough for me it will be good enough for them." Parents and teachers need to stay open-minded and to accept changes in popular culture, of which children are likely to be aware. Compromise is very important when dealing with objectics.

⇨　Establish a dictionary of "in" styles of dress, hair, jewelry, etc. Have your child create imaginary outfits based upon that dictionary and discuss the "meanings" of these outfits. In conjunction with this exercise, go through your child's clothing and talk about what each piece "says" and why.

Hygiene

⇨　Discuss generally, as well as specifically, the importance of personal hygiene as a mode of communication. Prepare a checklist or chart to record the hygiene activities for which your children take responsibility.

- Make a chart of hygiene responsibilities, complete with a frequency "key."
- Have the child write down the frequency with which he presently completes each task; for example, brushing teeth: twice a day.
- Talk about each item. For example, ask children, "Do you think you could manage to brush your teeth at least three times a day? If not, what about having a mint or sugarless gum at school?"
- Together with your child establish a set of guidelines for frequency and thoroughness of hygienic routines. You can reinforce progress with gold stars for younger children and praise for older children. Include activities such as:

washing hair	brushing teeth
changing underclothes	wearing clean clothes
washing face and hands	using deodorant
bathing	removing makeup

Cultural Objectics

⇨　Have children research cultural objectics for each continent. Here are some things to look for:

- national dress
- work clothes
- adaptations for climate and lifestyle
- decorative differences such as body painting, tattooing, teeth sharpening, etc.

Reward your child for a good project.

10

TEACHING AND REMEDIATION
FOR INDIVIDUAL CHILDREN

For additional practice in nonverbal language skills, you can use the following exercises to build on those provided thus far. These teaching and remediation exercises begin by focusing on particular emotions, then discuss these emotions as expressed in each of the six channels of nonverbal communication. The exercises can be repeated for many different emotions and altered or modified as needed.

Informal Teaching and Remediation—Emotions

➪ Work from the A to Z of Emotions on pages 180-181, writing down each item you would like to address with your child on an index card. Buy two inexpensive wallets or folders, or make some from construction paper. Label one "Positive Emotions" and the other "Negative Emotions."

Ask the child to decide if each card represents a positive or negative emotion. The child should then place the emotion card in the corresponding folder.

➪ Parents may choose to select one emotion each day or each week and discuss it thoroughly, producing a composite picture of that nonverbal emotion. Another option is to give the child one emotion a week along with a set number of exercises to complete, including the following:
  • Ask the child to give you three examples of situations which would incite the specific emotion. For example, if the emotion selected were fear, the child might give examples such as separation, strange dogs, thunder, dark, or monsters.
  • Ask the child to write down any alternative words for that emotion which reflect

its different intensities. (Fear: terror, surprise, nervousness, etc.) Ask the child how he or she would treat people feeling that way. (Hold their hand, reassure them, etc.)

Once the general aspects of the emotion have been discussed, the tutor and child can focus on the emotion as related to each of the six channels of nonverbal communication.

Focusing on the Six Channels of Nonverbal Communication

Ask children to choose an emotion (using the cards from the previous exercise, or asking the child to pick an emotion from the A to Z of Emotions). Then help them complete the following activities:

PARALANGUAGE

⇨ Name several ways people displaying the chosen emotion might sound. If the chosen emotion is "fear," what sort of paralinguistic clues might be present? For example, a wavering voice, a fast rate of speech, or stuttering might all signal fear.

⇨ Describe the tone of voice an afraid person might use. (High-pitched, sharp tone.)

⇨ Ask the child to suggest three different sentences that might be expressed when in that mood.

⇨ Using a tape recorder, state the emotion being portrayed ("This is a happy voice..."), and then ask the child to deliver the three sentences in an appropriate voice. Play the tape back and evaluate it for accuracy.

FACIAL EXPRESSIONS

⇨ List the common features of the chosen emotion in a facial expression.

⇨ Find an appropriate picture displaying that emotion.

POSTURE AND GESTURE

⇨ Describe how a person in this mood might stand.

⇨ Tell what nonverbal gestures are associated with a person in this mood. (For example: happy = thumbs up sign.)

SPACE AND TOUCH

⇨ Name ways that space might be important when dealing with a person feeling

this emotion. For example:
- angry = keep distance
- happy = come near

RHYTHM AND THE USE OF TIME
Use these exercises to help children become aware of rhythms and match them to emotions:

⇨ Vary the speed with which you tap your finger or make some other rhythmic noise and ask the child to tell you if the sounds are getting faster or slower. Ask which speed best communicates the emotion being studied.

⇨ Ask the child to match your rhythm variations with a sound-generating method of his or her own. For example, ask the child to clap or utter a vocal sound at a rate matching your finger tapping.

⇨ Talk with children about the rates of movement and activity of other people who feel the chosen emotion. Ask how these rates of behavior might reveal the emotions in question.

⇨ Have the child communicate other feelings through his or her rate of behavior. Ask the child to vary the speed of one task, such as building a tower of blocks or writing words on a chalkboard, to reveal different emotions.

⇨ Have the child match his or her rate of behavior with those of people that you observe together.

OBJECTICS
⇨ List any signs in our dress which indicate that we might be feeling a certain emotion. For example:
- sad = dark colors or rumpled clothes
- happy = bright colors

Cognitive Conflict

After completing this series, introduce some cognitive conflict (a tone of voice that does not match the verbal message being expressed). For example, if someone angrily yells "Have a good day," that person's tone of voice is in conflict with the verbal message; the speaker is thus sending two opposite messages at the same time.

⇨ Using a comic book or newspaper, read a passage using an inappropriate tone of voice; ask the child to determine which tone of voice and emotion would have been more correct for the subject matter. Repeat the same passage in the correct tone. The tutor can write a sentence and an emotion on cards to use instead of or along with the newspaper or comic book readings. For example: Read "Oh, what a lovely present," in a sad tone of voice, or "I'm going to fail this test!" in a happy tone of voice.

Cross-channeling

Activities or exercises that simultaneously reinforce skills in two or more nonverbal communication channels are called *cross-channeling*.

⇨ Show your child a picture of a very sad face, then ask how the person depicted would say the following sentence: "I'm going into my room now, but I'll be back later." Similarly, ask the child to portray the most likely posture of the person with the sad face.

⇨ Discuss postures or gestures that tell us about people's attitudes toward time.
- Tapping feet expresses impatience.
- Arms laced behind the head projects resting or laziness.
- Looking at a watch or clock repeatedly shows hurriedness.
Make a game of naming other nonverbal expressions of time attitudes.

⇨ Use the second hand on a clock to guide the child's rate of questioning or responding to questions.

⇨ Connect time with rhythm, and discuss occasions when it is important to take the time to go slowly and occasions when it is important to respond quickly.

⇨ Using the lotto base board on page 178, mix and match the nonverbal messages. This game will require some preparation prior to playing. You will need nine words or pictures for each of the nonverbal messages you are intending to test. Check that your child can use the appropriate paralanguage, posture, and/or gestures to indicate time, emotion, etc. For example, ask the child to match:
- facial expression with voice tone
- facial expression with appropriate posture
- facial expression with gesture
- gesture with emotion

⇨ Compile a list of situations where it is important to get nonverbal language correct. For example:

- being a good loser
- playing fair
- meeting someone for the first time
- coping with conflict situations

Ask children which aspects of nonverbal language they consider most important in each of these situations, and how they would use them to achieve the best effect.

⇨ As a fitting end to the exercises, select a variety of public places for the child to visit to practice his or her nonverbal skills. In keeping with the fun and reward element of the lessons, you may give the child a present at the end of each visit. Here are some favorite "field trip" locations:

- museum
- restaurant
- place of worship
- library
- theater
- cinema

(A visit to some of these venues, like a favorite restaurant or a special exhibit of dinosaurs, may be reward enough, and will be something that the child can look forward to.)

PART THREE

TEACHING
NONVERBAL LANGUAGE
AT SCHOOL

11

WHOLE CLASS APPROACHES

Many of the activities suggested for the individual in the preceding chapters are transferable to the classroom. Additional suggestions for whole class activities are presented below. Teachers are encouraged to alter or adapt them as they see fit.

Paralanguage

TEACHER PREPARATION

⇨ Review Chapter Four.

⇨ Discuss tone of voice with your class, emphasizing reference words like hard tone, soft tone, loud tone, and quiet tone before attempting these exercises.

⇨ Choose a nondescript sentence as a sample sentence. ("The cat is brown," for instance.) Use a tape recorder to record this sentence in a variety of tones of voice, making sure to include the basic happy, angry, sad, and frightened tones. Use different inflections, loudness of voice, and other paralinguistic elements to make your chosen emotions clear. Following the same steps, record a variety of speakers speaking in a variety of tones of voice. (Leave some silence in between your sentences as a cue to pause the tape when using it with the class.)

⇨ Create a worksheet with as many numbered blanks as emotions you choose to demonstrate.

⇨ Develop several simple scenarios that focus on paralinguistic communication. These situations can be formalized into a written play, described briefly in a paragraph or two, or conceptualized spontaneously during class discussion. For example, you could describe a scene in a crowded hallway between classes, write down a detailed conversation that takes place inside a church or synagogue during services, or briefly outline the subject matter of a telephone conversation between a child and a stranger or a child and a grandparent.

STUDENT PARTICIPATION

⇨ Play the recorded paralanguage test of the teacher's voice for the class. Play the entire tape through once so that the children can get a sense of the exercise as a whole.

⇨ Hand out the numbered sheet and ask the students to listen to the tape-recorded sentences again. Ask the children to write down the emotion being expressed in the appropriate worksheet blank. If you are dealing with a wide variety of emotions or difficult paralanguage cues, you can provide the class with a list of possible emotions from which to choose their answers.

The teacher can grade this exercise or review the appropriate responses with the class as a whole, according to the classroom's needs.

This exercise will reveal how well children can identify the basic emotions as well as the subtleties of expression through understanding paralanguage, and can be used both prior to nonverbal language training and after teaching and remediation efforts have begun. The children also learn the key elements of their teacher's happy, sad, angry, and serious voice tones in this exercise, which can make a difference in how they react to the teacher in the classroom.

⇨ After the class has mastered the teacher's varying tones of voice, play the tape of a variety of speakers. Ask the class to identify the emotions or meanings behind the tones of voice using a worksheet or responding orally to your questions.

⇨ Present to the students the series of situations you have developed or conceptualize the scenes through class discussion. Ask the pupils to suggest and discuss the tones of voice appropriate to each scenario. Then ask the students to role-play the situations using the appropriate tones of voice. For example, if the scenario is that someone has lost a dog, the children might suggest using a sympathetic or disappointed tone when speaking to the person.

⇨ For rate of speech exercises, refer to exercises for the individual in Chapter Four; these exercises can be adapted easily to the classroom setting.

Facial Expressions

TEACHER PREPARATION

➪ Review Chapter Five.

➪ Photocopy a variety of pictures of faces expressing emotions from the A to Z on pages 180-181. Label a folder or envelope "positive" and another "negative." Then label a series of index cards with the emotions you wish to focus on, using the A to Z of Emotions as a guide.

➪ The students can also make their own emotion cards for a personal reference pack, or the teacher may choose to make larger examples for wall displays. The advantage of children making their own sets of cards is that, at the end of an activity or exercise, they have packs which are useful later for games such as small group charades. (See page 99 for a description of charades.)

➪ Explain the idea of "common features" to the classroom. Before beginning these exercises, make sure the students understand the meaning of "positive" and "negative" as classifications for facial expressions. Also discuss the idea of "common features" and "horizontal zoning" with the children, drawing an outline of a face on the blackboard and explaining the three facial zones (see pages 62-63).

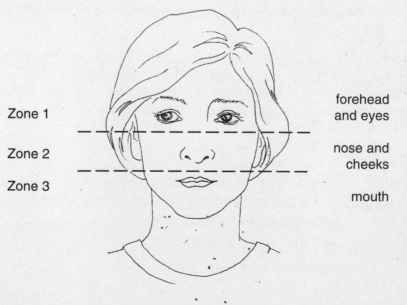

Zone 1 — forehead and eyes

Zone 2 — nose and cheeks

Zone 3 — mouth

STUDENT PARTICIPATION

⇨ Hand out the "emotion cards" and ask the students to decide whether their emotion cards are positive or negative. Ask them to put their card(s) in the appropriate "positive" or "negative" folders. The children can take turns walking to the front of the class to place their cards and explaining their emotions if time allows.

⇨ Distribute the photocopied facial expressions. Ask the students to categorize their worksheet faces as positive or negative. This exercise can identify those children who cannot tell the difference between positive and negative facial expressions.

⇨ Ask the children to apply an emotional label to each expression represented on the worksheet. This exercise reveals which words the child uses to describe an emotion, and consequently the intensity he or she attaches to it (for instance, upset, sad, or devastated).

⇨ Ask the students to mark the horizontal zones of each face. Front views, 45-degree views, side profile portraits, or a combination of the three can be depicted, depending on the skill level of the class.

⇨ Ask the students to study the same pictures further, then write down the common features for each emotion group. For instance, the children should list the common features of angry faces, then compose a separate list of common features for the happy faces, etc.

⇨ When the children have completed the worksheet, begin a class discussion where individuals can see how many of their peers chose similar features as common. For example, ask the children to raise their hands if they listed wide eyes as a common feature of an afraid face. Discrepancies discovered at this point will highlight facial expressions that are a problem for each individual.

⇨ The teacher (or individual children in turn) can select one positive and one negative emotion daily or weekly. The class can then discuss the emotion and practice both sending and receiving that expression facially. Role-playing can be a highly effective activity to use with this exercise.

Space and Touch

TEACHER PREPARATION
⇨ Review Chapter Six.

⇨ Create a wall chart or blackboard drawing of the communication zones on page 72.

⇨ Draw a silhouette of a person and mark various numbered locations on it; highlight areas both inside and outside the body line. This silhouette can be drawn on the blackboard or on a worksheet to be distributed to the students.

⇨ Create a worksheet of ten specific types of individuals (a stranger, teacher, bully, mother, friend, etc.) listed in one column, and ten different kinds of touches (a pat, shove, hug, handshake, etc.) listed in another column. Photocopy for distribution to the class.

⇨ Provide rulers or measuring tape.

STUDENT PARTICIPATION
⇨ Explain and discuss various types of space and touch with the students. Also discuss the various meanings of interpersonal distance and different kinds of touching.

⇨ Ask the children to measure the amount of personal space they have in the classroom, or measure around one student's desk as an example for the class.

⇨ Ask the children to make lists of all the places in the school where they have a great deal of space (like the gymnasium) and very little space (like the school lobby), using the classroom measurement as a point of comparison. This exercise should raise the children's awareness of locations of possible conflict—areas around the school where personal space is likely to be invaded.

⇨ List space and touch behavior that is unacceptable in the classroom (such as invading another's personal space or pushing).

⇨ Distribute worksheets listing individuals and types of touch. Ask the students to use the silhouette outline as a reference to decide the most appropriate place for each individual listed to touch the body with the type of touch specified.

Gestures and Postures

TEACHER PREPARATION

⇨ Review Chapter Seven.

⇨ Refer to the exercises for facial expression; the A to Z of Postures and Gestures can be used in a similar way. Practice demonstrating various postures and gestures.

⇨ Create a worksheet of drawings demonstrating different postures and gestures, including slouching, pointing, various batons, etc.

⇨ Create gesture and posture cards and positive and negative folders (see Facial Expressions section, page 143).

STUDENT PARTICIPATION

⇨ Discuss with students which gestures and postures are positive and which are negative.

⇨ Demonstrate various postures and gestures to the children to see what labels they attach to them without prior explanation.

⇨ Distribute posture and gesture worksheets. Ask the children to label and classify each drawing as positive or negative.

⇨ Ask students to place the posture and gesture cards in either the positive or negative envelopes, according to their classification.

⇨ Select one positive and one negative emotion to study daily or weekly.

⇨ Have students practice expressing and receiving various gestures and postures, using some of the activities described in earlier chapters as guidelines; role playing, especially in the form of charades, is very effective.

Rhythm and Time

TEACHER PREPARATION

⇨ Review Chapter Eight.

STUDENT PARTICIPATION

⇨ Discuss personal rhythm, punctuality, sequencing, time management, and other subjects relevant to your students.

⇨ Adapt individual exercises from Chapter Eight for use in the classroom.

Objectics

TEACHER PREPARATION
⇨ Review Chapter Nine.

⇨ Create index cards describing a type of dress or image, such as businesslike, smart, scruffy, on vacation, policeman, etc. Each image should be described identically on at least two cards. (The repeated images will allow a comparison of individual interpretations.) You may choose to bring in or create clothing or other props that relate to the images you choose to include on the cards.

⇨ Create a worksheet listing routine hygiene tasks (such as bathing, brushing teeth, changing undergarments, etc.) with blanks next to them, and a list of frequencies to choose from (daily, twice daily, once a week, etc.).

NOTE: Keep in mind that objectics is a difficult subject area to consider in the classroom. Conduct a discussion of objectics (using Chapter Nine as a guide) before attempting the following exercises.

STUDENT PARTICIPATION
⇨ Distribute the cards describing a type of dress or image to portray. Ask the students to dress like their card the following week. Children can come to school in their "disguise," bring clothes to dress up in for the assignment, or the teacher can provide props for the class to use.

⇨ Ask all the children representing a particular style to present themselves to the class. The teacher can ask each child to explain verbally why his or her choice of costume relates to the image he or she is portraying.

⇨ Discuss how appropriate the clothes are for the style given, and identify those attributes of the children's dress in the group that are similar or different.

⇨ Pass out the hygiene worksheet and ask the students to fill in the questionnaire. The questions should be filled out privately. Call out and discuss as a group the most appropriate answers to each question to avoid any individual embarrassment; each child then can consider in private his or her hygiene habits.

NOTE: Teachers should use their discretion with children who ask personal questions publicly as to whether it is more fitting to discuss the topic with the entire class or to discuss the issue individually at a more appropriate time. It should be emphasized to students that they can ask the teacher in private any questions they feel uncomfortable asking in front of the class.

12

A School-Based Curriculum for the Development of Nonverbal Language Skills

At DePaul School in Louisville, Kentucky, teaching the fundamentals of nonverbal communication has been part of the basic academic curriculum since 1989. What follows is the most recent curriculum used by DePaul School teachers and staff. It originated in the thinking of Sister Anne Rita Mouck and Peggy Harlowe and has been encouraged and sustained by the school's principal, Anthony Kemper. We wish to thank them and all the teachers and children at DePaul school for their efforts in the development of this curriculum and for their willingness to allow its publication here.

Because this curriculum is based on a system actually in use, this section can be used independently of this book. Once teachers become familiar with the concepts discussed in *Teaching Your Child the Language of Social Success*, they can select teaching plans described in the curriculum and implement them in the classroom. To make this easier, we have repeated some of the definitions of terms as well as exercises for group situations.

An Overview of Nonverbal Language

Introducing Students to Nonverbal Language

As children, we learned to speak, understand, and read the English language by breaking the "code" of the language—the alphabet. As we learned to receive and comprehend verbal communications, we also learned to express our feelings and desires by using words that others can understand. But even before that educational process began, we had to learn to "break" another "code"—the signals we call nonverbal communication.

Most information is not sent or received with words; it is conveyed through nonverbal communication. Nonverbal communication expresses desires, needs, an emotions without the use of words. It is a language that isn't taught in schools. We are simply expected to "know" how to interpret these messages as well as how to send them accurately. Some people have a nonverbal communication deficit, or disability, which causes them great difficulty socially. People who have a communication deficit are unable to use this unspoken language accurately to express themselves, and they are unable to receive and interpret the messages sent by others. (Just as dyslexia means a difficulty in reading, *dyssemia* means a difficulty in the exchange of nonverbal signals.) In order to be able to relate well to others, it is important that we know how to show emotions in an accurate way, through the use of facial expressions, gestures, spatial placement, and tone of voice.

One reason this is so important is because only about 10 percent of emotional meaning is expressed through words. Think of all the times your words contradict your true feelings. For example, if someone asks you, "How are you?" and you respond, "I'm great!" but have a sad look on your face, the message you sent verbally and the one you sent nonverbally contradict one another. This social skills class is designed to help students become accurate senders and receivers of this very important other language.

Before beginning instruction in this nonverbal communication unit, teach students the rules for working within a group. Begin each class with review and reinforcement of these rules.
  • Eyes must stay focused upon the teacher or on the person who is communicating with you.

- Hands must not obstruct the face or block the sound of words when you are trying to communicate.

During the first class session on nonverbal communication, use body language instead of words to convey instructions whenever you can. This will demonstrate to your students how people send messages nonverbally and how we must be alert in order to perceive and understand these messages correctly. Use hand signals to direct students as they enter the classroom. Point to where the students are to stand, sit, and place folders. Use gestures to direct students to keep their eyes on you. Begin each class session with a review of the many ways we send messages, by speaking, by writing, by using hand signals, or by facial expressions.

Discussion and Activities on Nonverbal Language

⇨ Familiarize students with the words in the following list. Present the vocabulary words with the use of a memory board and review them often.
  - language .... system used for communication
  - verbal.. spoken word
  - nonverbal .... unspoken
  - message... communication sent in various ways
  - communicate .... to send a message
  - send.. to give or to transmit
  - receive .... to get
  - sender .... one who communicates a message
  - receiver .... one who is being communicated with

⇨ Introduce your class to the various ways of sending and receiving messages, both verbally and nonverbally. Remind the students that there are many ways to communicate. Sometimes we communicate by speaking. Sometimes we communicate using our eyes, ears, and bodies. Ask the class to name various ways people express themselves or transmit information through the use of spoken or written communication. Some possible answers:
  - telephone
  - radio
  - computer
  - newspaper
  - letters
  - television
  - intercom system

⇨ Elicit other means of communicating from the students. Discuss sending a message through each medium and receiving a message through the same medium.
  - Ask students to think of ways people communicate without using words, such as gestures or motions, facial expressions, or sounds like whistling or humming.

- Reiterate that messages are both sent and received. Have students practice being both sender and receiver with the communication methods just discussed.

PARALANGUAGE

Clarification of the Skill

Paralanguage deals with the *sound* of language, not the words used in verbal language. Usually the sound which accompanies the words is much more indicative of the true feelings of the speaker than the actual words spoken. Using a telephone or listening to the radio illustrates the importance of paralanguage.

Paralanguage is divided into four areas:
- sound patterns
- speed of talking
- intensity of speech
- different tones of voice

Paralanguage refers to all aspects of sound which communicate emotion. People who can accurately "read" sounds gain instant feedback concerning the emotional state of the sender, and they can then respond appropriately. People who cannot pick up on these nonverbal sound clues may respond inappropriately or inaccurately.

Introducing Students to Paralanguage

Paralanguage is the only channel of nonverbal language we can "hear"; the other nonverbal channels are seen. It includes elements such as tone, loudness, intensity of voice, and sounds like humming or whistling that are uttered between words. We have all asked someone if anything was wrong and heard them respond "no," but we could tell by the sound of the answer that the words did not represent the person's true state of mind. Instead of believing what the person said, we believed the paralinguistic message—the *sound* of what was said.

Discussion and Activities on Paralanguage

SOUND PATTERNS
⇨ For infants, the only means of communicating needs or feelings is through the medium of sounds. As people grow older, they still use this means as a way of communicating, but in a more sophisticated way. People can indicate that food tastes good by saying "ummmm!" We can also use sounds to conveys fear or

warning. Ask students to name sounds that express these thoughts or feelings.

- "I don't like the taste of this food."
- "Watch out, don't do that."
- "I don't know, let me see."
- "Nonsense!"
- "Oh, I'm sorry to hear that."
- "That is disgusting!"

⇨ Sounds can also irritate. For instance, consider the person who says "um" every other word in a sentence, or the person who disturbs others with a loud or grating laugh. People who are nervous often continually clear their throat, and that, too, can be annoying. Ask the students to think of vocal sounds that can irritate a listener.

NOTE: These examples remind us how common such sounds are and how difficult social interaction would be for a child who could not understand the messages sent by these sounds. Receptive dyssemia makes it impossible to respond appropriately to sound messages.

SPEED OF TALKING

How fast or how slowly we talk sends a nonverbal message. To speak very quickly can indicate several different things; we may feel an urgency about what we are saying, we may be letting others know we have a lot of information to share, or we may feel nervous. There are appropriate times to speak rapidly. When we have limited time and a lot to say, or when we see that the person we are speaking to is in a hurry, we speed up our speech. There are also inappropriate times to speak rapidly. When we are trying to explain or teach something, we normally slow our rate of speech. In general conversation, the speed of speech should be moderate. The key is to be able to perceive our rate of speed and moderate it to *fit the circumstance*.

⇨ Ask students to name occasions when slow speech or fast speech would be appropriate.

⇨ Have the students listen to various statements while turned away from the speaker, then ask them to determine the situation conveyed by the speaker by the rate of speed used to communicate. For instance, "Let's go to the store" could be said with moderate speed to indicate a casual need, but at a rapid pace, the same sentence could indicate urgency and a need to hurry.

⇨ Ask students to role-play circumstances which would require various rates of speed in talking.
- a hurried mother trying to answer a question while preparing a meal
- a person giving a speech to a group of people

- a teacher explaining a math problem to students
- a student explaining to a teacher why his homework was not turned in on time
- a father explaining to a child why it is wrong to lie
- two people having a friendly casual conversation

⇨ Repeat the same kind of role-play as in the previous exercise, but this time have the students give a response, synchronizing their rate of speed to that of the speaker. This requires both receptive and expressive skills.

⇨ Ask students to role-play a situation where a person is unable to synchronize his rate of speed with the person he is talking with and constantly interrupts the speaker. This exercise should make the students aware of appropriate timing when having a conversation or discussion.

Variation In Speech

⇨ It is important to know that the emphasis we put on certain words conveys a strong message. Ask students to listen to a sentence as you read it with the stress on different words and have them explain how emphasis affects the meaning.

- <u>You</u> may not go. .... Everyone else may go but you.
- You <u>may</u> not go. .... There is just a possibility that you will not be able to go. Or: You are not given permission to go.
- You may <u>not</u> go. .... You are definitely not allowed to go.
- You may not <u>go</u>. .... You cannot go; stay right where you are.

⇨ Ask the students to practice emphasizing different words in a sentence, then describe how the meaning of the sentence alters as they vary the emphases.

Tone Of Voice

Perhaps the most powerful communicator in nonverbal language is tone of voice. Compare the comforting tone of voice a mother uses with a sick child, saying, "You'd better go to bed now" with the sharp tone she uses when the child has been misbehaving: "You'd better go to bed <u>now</u>!" Children who are unable to receive and express messages, whether subtle or overt, can become social outcasts. Many people are unaware of the appropriate tone of voice to use in certain situations. Often they will sound angry or hostile when they are really attempting to be friendly. This aspect of nonverbal communication, because of the subtlety involved and the many variations required by different circumstances, is an enigma to people who suffer from receptive and expressive dyssemia.

NOTE: It requires a great amount of time and many concrete examples to teach students the skill of accurate interpretation of tone of voice. First, create an awareness of tone of voice in the students; then follow up with in-depth discussion.

⇨ Before class, prepare a supply of sentences and situations to use in these exercises. You can write them on the blackboard or on slips of paper for the students to draw at random.

⇨ Give examples of how tone of voice can alter the meaning of words. Have the students practice placing different meanings onto various words simply by changing their tone of voice.

⇨ Have a student say a sentence you have provided in a tone of voice which expresses a particular feeling. The student may then select another student to interpret the meaning of the tone of voice used.

⇨ Give students particular situations and ask that they use the appropriate tone of voice to respond to them. (If the situation were "Mary lost her wallet," the student should respond in a tone of voice showing concern or compassion.)

⇨ Help students learn the difference between sincere and insincere tones of voice.

⇨ Help students become aware of the possibility of a discrepancy between the meaning of what is said and the way it is said.

⇨ Play a video tape, choosing a segment that demonstrates tone of voice. Have the students interpret the emotions or intent of the speaker.

⇨ Discuss with the students appropriate tones and voice levels of laughter in specific situations. Often, people with voice tone expressive dyssemia laugh too long and loud over something not exceedingly funny. Ask students to name occasions when a slight smile, a soft giggle, or a full laugh would be appropriate. Discuss times when laughter would be rude or hurtful.

FACIAL EXPRESSIONS

Clarification of the Skill

People respond quickly to facial expressions. Because they are instantly received and because other aspects of body language may be more subtle, facial expressions are one of the most significant message senders. People's faces give us valuable clues about their feelings and attitudes. In order to read body language it is essential to be visually aware of those with whom we interact. To read the messages being sent through facial expressions, it is necessary to have eye contact with the person we are speaking to. Usually people who have difficulty maintaining eye contact when they are speaking also have trouble maintaining eye contact when they are listening. Lack of eye contact can be interpreted by others as low self-esteem, dishonesty, or lack of intelligence, and can put a person at a disadvantage in social interaction.

Introducing Students to Facial Expression

We have all heard phrases like "Her face fell," and "He's down in the mouth." When we feel "up," our facial muscles also go up (in a smile) and our eyes lift. When we feel "down," our whole body sags and our facial muscles drop. We exchange a constant stream of information about our attitudes and feelings through our facial expressions. To interact successfully with others we must know how to read faces accurately and how to produce facial expressions that clearly convey our feelings.

Discussions and Activities on Facial Expression

A full discussion of "emotions" ensures that students understand each emotion's meaning as well as the circumstances that might evoke that emotion. Students with such an understanding will be better able to demonstrate emotions facially. It is crucial that each student have an opportunity to participate actively in these exercises. Some will not be able to recognize and mimic the facial expressions, and some will be able to recognize the expression but not mimic it. These findings will indicate receptive facial dyssemia, expressive dyssemia, or both. Before proceeding to any other instruction, students must be able to recognize similar and different facial expressions. Devote as much time as necessary to these exercises until the students are proficient.

⇨ Discuss the importance of using eye contact when speaking or listening. People form very definite opinions about us when we use good eye contact as well as when we do not. When you have something important to say and really want people to listen to you, be sure to look them right in the eyes. You will then be more likely to keep their attention and appear knowledgeable and sincere. If you look away from people when you are talking with them, it is almost impossible to hold their attention.

⇨ Ask students to set a goal to train themselves to have eye contact with others. At first, they might find it difficult, but once they get into the habit of good eye contact, it will become much easier. Teach them the difference between appropriate eye contact and staring.

⇨ Discuss and define emotions such as sadness, anger, compassion, fear, happiness, and disgust. Ask students how they would define each emotion and what would cause someone to feel the emotion.

⇨ Ask the students to make a face illustrating a specific feeling while they look in a mirror. Emphasize to the students that they must be able to express as well as read facial messages. Place special emphasis on facial expressions that convey anger. Many students are unable to discriminate between a serious or sad face and an angry face.

NOTE: It is of primary importance that students be made aware of any deficiency in reception or expression of facial "language." Lack of variety in facial expression ("monotonic" facial expression) gives the expression of dullness or low intelligence. Instruction in this area will probably require a great deal of time.

⇨ Students often lack adequate social skills when being introduced to someone. Role-play introductions using cross-channeling—practicing facial expression, eye contact, spatial placement and body language together (see page 136). Alter this exercise by role-playing conversations with adults in a variety of situations using several nonverbal skills.

⇨ Ask the students to sit in a circle. Each student takes a turn to make a facial expression which expresses an emotion. All of the other students must imitate that expression. This exercise demonstrates whether or not students are able to facially duplicate a particular emotion. Then ask the students to respond to that facial expression appropriately.

⇨ Set up a classroom situation in which you demonstrate different emotions through facial expressions, such as serious, relaxed, disturbed, etc., and ask students to determine those attitudes.

⇨ Select a topic for discussion. Ask students one at a time to display the proper facial expression while discussing the topic with you. Change the subject of discussion as you work with different students.

⇨ Give the students sentences to read and ask them to make the appropriate facial expressions as they speak. Possible sentences: "I am going to have a test tomorrow and I am afraid I won't pass," or "Mr. Tate, I am sorry that I talked out in your class yesterday, and I will work on having better behavior today," or "Miss Jones, could you please help me, I don't understand what my directions are."

⇨ Play a game called "facial expression telephone."
1. Seat students in a circle.
2. Have one student turn to the student in the next chair and express an emotion using only the face.
3. This student then turns to the next student, sharing the same facial expression.
4. After the students have passed the expression around the circle, ask the first student how accurate the final expression is.
5. Repeat this exercise but ask the students to shield the sides of their faces with their hands so that only their neighbor can see the facial expression.

⇨ Play the "circle game." (This game can also be played using gestures.)
1. Have students sit in a circle
2. Go around the circle, asking each student to pick a different emotion, then to make a facial expression that shows that emotion.
3. One student starts the game by naming again the emotion he or she picked and making the corresponding facial expression.
4. That student then selects from memory another student's stated emotion and makes the facial expression corresponding to that emotion.
5. The first player to identify correctly what and whose emotion is being demonstrated calls out the emotion and the student who chose it.
6. The student who calls out the correct emotion and student continues the game by recalling another student's emotion and facial expression (from memory), then reproducing that facial expression.
7. Again, the first student to call out the emotion being expressed and the student who originally chose it get to continue the game.

SPACE AND TOUCH

THE CONCEPT OF SPACE

Clarification of the Skill

The space around people plays a major role in communication. Help students learn about the rules that govern people's space so that they can interact appropriately. There are several kinds of space involved in nonverbal communication.

Territorial space refers to the structures which we inhabit—our room, our house, our yard, our neighborhood. Territorial space is not usually portable.

Personal space is the area immediately in front of, behind, and beside a person. We carry this space around with us. It is portable and always with us. We put much more emphasis on the importance of personal space than we do on territorial space.

Personal mental space refers to subject matters we consider private. Everyone has a personal mental space which others must honor. Personal questions and comments make many people uncomfortable. We must learn that there are topics of conversation, questions, and comments that can cause embarrassment or uneasiness to others.

Discussion and Activities on Territorial Space

⇨ Describe territorial space as space we make personal claims on, but which does not move around with us. Discuss examples such as a house and the yard which surrounds it, the desk the students sit in at school, or their seat in a church or movie theater. Animals are very possessive of their "territory" and will go to great lengths to guard and protect it. Humans view territorial space in much the same way. Give examples of how both animals and humans mark their territory and how they defend it when threatened. Here are some topics for discussion.
  • the student's room in the home
  • the student's desk at school
  • the student's yard at home
  • the student's place standing in line
  • games which require defense of territory
  • getting lunches and coats in and out of storage places
  • ways humans mark and defend territorial space (e.g., fences and walls)
  • instances when countries go to war over territorial space, either to protect or expand it

⇨ Ask students to role-play the following situations:
  • One student assumes the role of a young person while another student assumes the role of a parent. The child notices a person driving by his or her house several times. After noticing the same car pass by the house very slowly and even stopping in front of it, the child runs to his or her parent to call attention to the car. The child then describes the situation to the parent and explains why the car's actions make him or her apprehensive.
  • One student assumes the role of a young person standing in a line at school or at a movie, another assumes the role of a "line-breaker." The second person invades the child's territory, moving the child out of his space and taking

his place in line. Demonstrate a discussion between the two about the invasion of a territorial space.

- Two students are seated in desks at school. One student reaches into the other student's desk and takes out a library book. Role-play how such an action is perceived as an invasion of territorial space and act out the emotions that result from this action.
- Two children are playing baseball in the back yard. The ball is thrown into a neighbor's fenced yard. How can the children retrieve it in a way that would not be an invasion of the neighbor's territorial space?

Discussion and Activities on Personal Space

Personal space plays a greater role in the teaching of nonverbal language than does territorial space. Help the students focus on the importance of respecting others' personal space.

⇨ Talk about situations that concretely define what is meant by personal space, such as waiting in line, sitting at the lunch table, or working together seated at tables. Allow students to express how they feel when someone invades their space; verbalizing such feelings will help them more fully understand the concept of personal space. Then, have the students discuss how they invade others' personal space and the ensuing negative results.

⇨ Discuss the fact that there are social "rules" in our dealings with others. People who seem to be oblivious to these rules and frequently break these unwritten laws may be considered "weird." How we place ourselves spatially with others is an important part of acceptable interaction with others. If we stand too close to another person when we talk, the person feels uncomfortable and tries to back away. People who have trouble reading such signals and continue unacceptable spatial placement will have problems with social interaction. If we spread our things into other people's space at a table, or invade their space with our bodies, they resent us. When personal space is invaded, problems can arise.

⇨ Ask the students to recall instances when their personal space has been violated and their reactions to the invasion. Also ask them to think of instances when they have invaded other people's personal space and the resulting consequences.

⇨ Ask the class to observe some everyday examples of using personal space, like standing in line, walking on stairways, or sitting in groups.

It is important to know that some people have difficulty receiving spatial messages, some people have difficulty sending spatial messages, and some people have trouble both sending and receiving these spatial, nonverbal messages. First, we need to learn to be careful about infringing on other people's space, and second, we need to remember that some people who violate our space may not be aware that they are breaking a social "rule." Sometimes it might be helpful to respond tactfully to such infringements by saying courteously, "I feel uncomfortable when you stand so close."

Activities for Practicing Personal Space Usage

After thoroughly discussing and demonstrating personal space, follow up with practical application. The following suggestions will assist in concretizing the concept of personal space for the students. Your goal as the teacher is to lead them to understand the need to allow each person enough space for comfort in various settings.

⇨ Have students discuss or role-play the following situations:
  - Standing in line: Encourage students to remember that when standing in line, whether to enter a bus, a cafeteria, or a classroom, the "me-first" concept is foolish and often counterproductive. Everyone will eventually gain admittance, and pushing and crowding will only slow everyone down. Repeat demonstrations of this concept to help students internalize these ideas.
  - Sitting next to someone in a crowded situation, such as an assembly, a movie, an airplane: Discuss with students the ways they can avoid infringing on another person's personal space.
  - Working with others in a crowded area: Discuss how students can work or play games together without taking up another's space.
  - Sitting in a classroom: Talk about the territorial and personal space issues that arise when students are sitting at their desks.

⇨ Discuss the spatial etiquette for these situations.
  - placing and/or retrieving articles from lockers or racks
  - using the drinking fountain
  - standing next to the person with whom you are talking
  - sitting next to a person you do not know
  - standing at a bus stop next to strangers
  - using the stairway

⇨ Seat the students at a work table or cafeteria table with books and paper or games in front of them. Demonstrate how to define personal space in this kind of situation. You may want to help them visualize this concept by using tape to define each child's own personal space. It is important to teach students that when they infringe upon personal space, it is socially correct to apologize and say "excuse me." Ask the students to role-play several different scenarios illustrating acceptable and unacceptable spatial placement.

⇨ Set up a situation where two groups of students are going in opposite directions but using the same doorway. Demonstrate techniques to use in a congested area.

⇨ Demonstrate actions or gestures people make to indicate someone is invading their personal space. Teach the student to be aware of the reactions of people whose personal space has been violated. Messages people send when others get too close include backing away, giving a "look," or reacting angrily. Many students with receptive and/or expressive spatial dyssemia do not read these signals.

Discussion and Activities on Personal Mental Space

People feel possessive not only about their physical space but also about their mental space. We "rope off" certain private and personal topics; we feel uneasy when people invade this space by asking questions or making inappropriate comments. People who have difficulty sending and receiving nonverbal messages will have difficulty choosing appropriate topics of conversation; they will also be unable to receive the message that they have "overstepped their bounds" in their choice of topics. There are many subjects which should be avoided in general social conversations, such as detailed questions about one's family or financial situation. When we step into the "forbidden territory" of someone's mental space, we can usually read the warning if we are aware of what to look for. These signals vary widely. When we ask a question or make a comment that prompts a sharp retort, a change of subject, or a mumbled, reluctant answer, we know to drop the subject. Remind students that they should usually avoid discussing personal things or asking personal questions of people older than themselves or people that they don't know well.

⇨ Ask students to role-play the following situations:
  • Jack, a ten-year-old boy, comes home from school to find a cleaning lady he has not met before. He introduces himself and begins to ask her personal

questions concerning her family and how much money she makes. She lowers her voice, averts her eyes and mumbles an answer. Jack keeps asking these questions until she finally tells him she would rather not discuss her personal life with him.

- Janie and Beth are best friends. Beth constantly questions Janie about what Janie writes in her diary. Finally, Janie tells Beth that a diary is a personal and private matter and she resents being questioned about it.
- Bob asks his teacher, Mr. Stewart, many questions about his age and his family. The teacher takes him aside and explains that it is not appropriate for a child to ask an adult personal questions.

⇨ Follow up the role-playing with a discussion of how to send, how to read, and how to respond to signals relating to personal mental space.

Discussion and Activities on the Four Spatial Zones

When teaching about the nonverbal skill of space usage, it is helpful to introduce the concept of "zones." We can think of the space around us as divided into four "conversational zones," or four areas within which certain kinds of communications are appropriate. Just as we are expected to slow down in a school zone, we are expected to behave certain ways in each conversation zone. These zones are:

- the intimate zone
- the social zone
- the personal zone
- the public zone

Becoming familiar with these zones will help us learn how to place ourselves when we converse with one or more people.

THE INTIMATE ZONE

The intimate zone is different from personal space. Your personal space moves around with you; it is your own personal "comfort zone." Different people may require different amounts of personal space. The intimate zone, however, is a fixed area; within this zone only certain kinds of communication are appropriate. We permit family and close friends into the intimate zone. A lowered tone is used in this zone, and intimate or personal issues may be appropriately discussed here. This zone begins at nearly touching distance and extends out about eighteen inches. There are some exceptions to this zone. There are occasions when those other than family or close friends may enter—for example, a doctor or nurse, a teacher speaking with a student about a serious matter, or a coach working with a player.

⇨ Have students walk the parameters of the zones as you discuss them so they can visualize the distances you are describing. Some students may not be able to estimate distances.

⇨ Have students discuss and demonstrate who would be allowed in their intimate zone as well as who should not be allowed to enter this zone. Discuss and demonstrate when it is permissible for the student to enter another person's intimate zone.

NOTE: It is important that students understand when it is appropriate to use the intimate zone and when it is *not* appropriate to use it. It is also important that they realize that *they* have the right to control who is allowed into their intimate zone.

THE PERSONAL ZONE

In most everyday settings, people conduct conversations with friends and acquaintances in the personal zone. The *personal zone* extends from approximately eighteen inches to four feet. A normal speaking tone is used in this zone.

⇨ Discuss with students who is acceptable and who is not acceptable in the personal zone. Ask them to name circumstances when they should not enter another person's personal zone. Help them compile a list of people who should not enter their personal zone uninvited. Talk about polite ways to discourage others from entering the personal zone.

⇨ Ask students to role-play situations that illustrate proper and improper use of the personal zone in everyday settings.
  • talking with a friend on the playground
  • eating with friends at a restaurant
  • talking with other students during a break in the classroom
  • talking with a teacher about schoolwork
  • greeting a complete stranger
  • speaking with the school nurse about a problem
During role-play have students pay special attention to the distance between them and other people.

THE SOCIAL ZONE

People that we have just met, or are about to meet, would stand within the social zone. The social zone ranges from approximately four to twelve feet. We interact with people in this zone when we attend classes, parties, or dances, school functions, sports events, and church or synagogue services. We usually talk with friends or acquaintances in this zone, but there are occasions when we encounter complete strangers there. As a rule, we carry on only general conversation within the social zone. It is inappropriate to discuss private or personal matters in this area because others could also be within hearing distance and able to observe and overhear. A moderately loud tone of voice is typically acceptable in this area, but circumstances in this zone should dictate the volume of voice.

⇨ Have students role-play appropriate usage of this zone in various situations.
  • A child at a large party with his parents begins to publicly discuss a recent family matter, such as a financial problem. The parent reminds the child that it is not appropriate to talk about private family matters with such a voice level and at such a distance.
  • Recreate any situations involving social distance that have caused conflict in your classroom.

THE PUBLIC ZONE
The public zone is the largest area, starting at about twelve feet away and extending indefinitely. We generally do not communicate verbally within this zone, but instead use gestures and facial expression, waiting until we are within the social zone to have conversations. It is usually not acceptable to communicate loudly with someone within this zone. There are locations where the public zone can be constricted to a smaller space, as in an elevator.

⇨ Have students role-play how to communicate within this zone in various situations. Emphasize the use of good social judgment in choosing a voice level. Allow students to place themselves without advance coaching. After the role-playing is over, discuss and demonstrate the appropriate spatial placement and voice level with the students.
  • greeting an acquaintance from a great distance
  • speaking with a friend in a movie theater
  • talking with friends at a small social gathering
  • having a conversation with a relative sitting across from you in an office waiting room

⇨ Pretend a church or movie is empty, except for one person who is a stranger to the person entering. Ask a student to enter and decide where it is socially unacceptable to take a seat. (After role-playing, establish the fact that it would be socially unacceptable to take a seat too close to the stranger.)

⇨ Ask students to pretend they are on an elevator. Where should they look? If they are on the elevator with both strangers and a friend, what voice volume would be appropriate? What type of conversation would be socially acceptable? Where should they stand in relation to other people?

THE CONCEPT OF TOUCH

Clarification of the Skill

There are different kinds of touch, such as patting, squeezing, stroking, and brushing. How we touch or are touched communicates a message, sometimes positive and sometimes negative. Touch can communicate praise, compassion, anger, and many other feelings. For instance, patting indicates approval whereas poking is a threatening or a punishing touch. Because we invade personal space when we touch another person, society has made certain rules involving touching. It is usually permissible to touch someone lightly on the outside of certain areas on the body line, such as the outside of the arm or leg, or on the shoulder, especially if we accompany the touch with words like "excuse me." It is considered improper or even threatening to touch on the inside of the body line. For example, to move a person from one place to another by simply placing your hands on the outside of the arms or on the shoulder is a nonthreatening, guiding gesture, but to place your hands around a person's arm violates personal space and appears threatening. Hugging is usually a sign of affection, but American rules of touch dictate that it is socially unacceptable to hug someone you have not met or just recently met, or someone who is not a close member of the family or a personal friend.

NOTE: Expressive touch can convey all sorts of emotions. It is important that we as educators keep the rules of touching in mind as we work with our students. It is almost never acceptable to touch a child roughly, to put our hands on a student's face, or to "poke" a student. We must be extremely cognizant of the fact that children are very sensitive to a teacher's touch—the message a teacher sends through touch should be negative or threatening only when absolutely necessary.

Discussion and Activities on Touch

⇨ Demonstrate the inappropriateness of touching someone you don't know or are not closely associated with. Have students role-play a situation in which two students who are not close friends are standing in line next to each other. One student pokes or puts a hand on the other. It is important for the students to realize that they *never* touch—or permit themselves to be touched by—anyone they don't know or don't know well. Explain that there are very specific "rules" in society for touching. Make the students aware that they have the *right* to determine who touches them, just as others have the same right which must be respected.

⇨ Demonstrate the different types of touch. Is poking acceptable? How does the one being poked usually respond? In which situations would stroking be acceptable? Which emotion does shaking someone usually communicate? Is putting your feet on another person or kicking ever acceptable? What message does each kind of touch send and what response does it elicit?

BODY LANGUAGE: POSTURE AND GESTURE

Clarification of the Skill

We often communicate through our postures and gestures. We are constantly sending and receiving messages by using our head, arms, legs, fingers, and shoulders. Our body language conveys feeling. For example, when we feel "up" our whole body goes up. The shoulders, eyebrows, eyes, and lips reach "up" to smile! When we feel "down" the whole body goes "down." The shoulders droop, as well as the facial muscles. We need to learn to be aware of our own body language and also how to accurately interpret signals sent by someone else's body language.

Discussion and Activities on Posture

Posture is a forceful nonverbal communicator. Posture indicates feelings, commitment, and attitude, up close and also from a distance. We communicate constantly by our posture whether we intend to or not. It is crucial that we not only send accurate messages, but also interpret correctly the messages we receive in this way.

⇨ Review the terms *receive, send, sender, receiver, communicate,* and *message,* and introduce these new ones:
  • language ......a system for sending and/or receiving information
  • gesture ....a body movement that expresses a feeling or idea
  • posture ....the position or carriage of the body or parts of the body

⇨ Make a list of the "up" and "down" body language people use to express emotions—raising or lowering eyebrows, "hanging" your head, or "keeping your chin up." Collect common phrases that illustrate this kind of body language, such as being "stuck up," "having your head in the clouds," feeling "down in the mouth," or "feeling low." Concrete examples will help students understand the concept.

⇨ Ask younger students to identify and locate the following body parts:
- face
- hands
- arms
- eyes
- head
- shoulders
- eyebrows
- eyelids

⇨ Discuss and define the following emotions:
- sadness
- anger
- seriousness
- disgust
- fear
- happiness
- relief
- disappointment

⇨ Explain to the students that arms, hands, and fingers can be used like a baton to send many kinds of messages. Discuss and demonstrate these common gestures.

FINGER SILENT SIGNALS
- crooking index finger .... come here
- finger to lips .... be quiet
- pointing .... pay attention
- index finger to thumb sign .... everything's okay
- finger across throat .... stop, or I'm in trouble
- tapping finger .... hurry up

ARMS AND HANDS SILENT SIGNALS
- arms on hips .... impatience, determination
- arm extended and palm out .... stop
- arm extended .... don't come near me
- arms crossed over the chest .... closed off, not receptive
- arm around someone's shoulder ...... offering friendship or comfort
- clenched fist .... anger, threat
- shaking a finger .... chastising, warning
- waving .... hello, goodbye
- crooking index finger .... come here
- hands extended, palms down in front of body, moving hands up and down slightly .... slow down, quiet down

POSTURE SILENT SIGNALS
- standing with legs apart and hands on hips .... aggression, anger
- sitting or standing erect, possibly leaning forward somewhat, with eyes straight forward .... enthusiasm, energy

- standing hunched over, looking
  aside or backwards .... fear
- chin raised, hands on hips,
  staring arrogantly ahead .... defiance
- slouching, hands in pockets,
  looking around .... boredom
- head down, kicking foot on floor .... defeat
- shoulders high, hands in "ready
  position" on hips, looking straight
  ahead .... confidence
- head down or in hand, fluttering
  hands, moving about rapidly, gaze
  averted from other person .... stress, worry
- comfortably situated in sitting
  position, slouched slightly, resting
  face .... rest, relaxation
- standing, tapping a foot .... impatience

⇨ Make sure that all students are able to send and receive the messages sent by different body language signals. This can be accomplished in various ways:
  - The teacher whispers to a selected sender which of the above messages to send to a chosen receiver. The receiver then states the message conveyed by the gesture or posture of the sender.
  - A student picks an index card with a message written on it. The student then pantomimes the message to a specified receiver or to the group as a whole; the teacher selects one student to interpret the message verbally.

⇨ Divide students into small groups; ask each group to create and role-play a situation that illustrates one of the gestures or postures described above. This exercise in-sures that students understand when it is appropriate or standard to use certain types of body language.

NOTE: Use full-length mirrors during this instruction in order to help students see how messages are sent and received through body language. Very often people are unaware of how they look to others, as well as what the looks of others are intended to express!

⇨ Show students pictures depicting different gestures or postures. Have the students identify and discuss the message indicated in each picture. Expand the game by naming a feeling, emotion, or message and asking the students to choose a corresponding picture.

⇨ Ask the students to take turns assuming a posture at their desks. Have the other students decide what message is being sent to the classroom teacher or to other students in the class.

⇨ Ask the students to role-play the following situation: a student is speaking with a teacher about a problem or asking a question about class while standing in a negative posture. The teacher responds unfavorably because of the message sent by that posture. Repeat the exercise, but this time ask the student to assume a posture denoting interest and energy and ask the person playing the teacher to respond appropriately.

RHYTHM AND TIME

RHYTHM

Clarification of the Skill

When we work and live with those whose rhythm, or pace of life, is different from ours, we often feel uncomfortable. Some people think, react and move quickly, and others are more laid back and unhurried. People with a fast rhythm may lose patience when others prefer a slower pace; people with a slow rhythm may feel nervous around those with a faster pace. If we are out of "sync" with others, we can feel uncomfortable.

Discussion and Activities on Rhythm

⇨ Explain to students that by learning to "read" and respond to the rhythm of other people, they will be able to communicate with them more easily. Introduce and discuss the following terms:
  • rhythm .... a regular pattern of movement
  • receptive use of rhythm .... recognition of the rhythms of others and knowing what they mean
  • expressive use of rhythm .... ability to adjust our rhythm to the rhythm

⇨ Begin by using rhythmic exercises to increase the awareness of rhythmic pacing. For example:
  • vary the rate of hand clapping and have the student match your rhythmic clap

- practice speaking at varying rates and have the student match your rhythm
- walk at varying speeds and have the student adjust the pace to match yours

⇨ Have students role-play situations in which they must match their rates of rhythmic speeds to accommodate others, either verbally or physically.

⇨ Provide video tapes of demonstrations of varying rhythms in speaking and walking for the students to discuss and mimic. (These videos could be taped television shows.)

⇨ Ask students to role-play situations which demonstrate the comfort and discomfort levels produced by being "in sync" or "out of sync" with others.

⇨ Discuss when it would be appropriate to move at a slow rate of speed and at a faster rate of speed. Have one student provide a situation, then choose another student to demonstrate how to respond with an appropriate corresponding rate of walking or talking.

SITUATIONS FOR A SLOW RATE OF SPEED
- walking in church
- changing classes
- walking with a large group of people in a mall

SITUATIONS FOR A FAST RATE OF SPEED
- walking to catch a bus
- taking part in a fire drill
- hurrying to complete a task or reach a destination
- responding to an emergency situation

⇨ Discuss "family rhythm." Ask the students to think of times in a family situation when the pace picks up—when parents rush to complete tasks before company comes, when the family is hurrying to reach a destination, or when parents and children hurry to leave the house on time for school. Remind students that at such times they need to be aware of the rhythm of their family and adjust their pace accordingly. These are *not* appropriate times for discussing a lengthy problem or dawdling over a task.

TIME

Clarification of the Skill

Our use or abuse of time is one way we communicate to others. We often judge or form opinions of each other according to the way we use time. We can honor commitments, express feelings, and communicate respect and caring by the way we use time. People don't usually realize the importance of the use of time until someone breaks one of the rules of this form of communicating. We speak this nonverbal language every day, so it is important that we learn to receive and express its signals accurately. Students are constantly sending messages by their use of time. If they do not learn the proper expressive use of time, they may unintentionally send negative messages to others.

Discussion and Activities on Use of Time

⇨ Before beginning the exercises, review the terms *receptive* and *expressive* with the students:
- receptive use of time .... understanding how others use time to communicate
- expressive use of time .... the use of time to communicate to others

⇨ Use the following situations to illustrate correct *receptive* uses of time. These examples indicate a sensitivity on the part of the *receiver* to the importance of time. Lead students in a discussion and then clarify and reinforce their understanding by having them role-play each situation.
- Before leaving home for the afternoon, a mother tells her daughter to stay in the house until she telephones her at three o'clock. The call doesn't come at three, but the child is aware that she should wait until it does come before leaving the house.
- The teacher gives an assignment to be completed by a certain date. She indicates that the student should spend two hours per night preparing the assignment. The student is able to perceive that this assignment is a significant one and time is an important factor in this situation. (Receptive use of time.) The student is diligent and prompt in completing the task. What message would the student send to the teacher if the assignment were turned in late? What message did the student send by doing the assignment on time and turning it in to the teacher on time? (Expressive use of time.)
- A parent has just arrived home from work and is extremely busy trying to

171

prepare dinner for the family. The child senses and receives the message that this is not the time to approach the parent with an involved conversation.

- A student stops by after school to talk with a teacher. The teacher looks at his watch several times. The student "receives" the message that the teacher's time is limited and asks for an appointment so they can continue the conversation later.

⇨ Use the following situations to teach *expressive* uses of time. They illustrate an understanding of how to send correct signals through the use of time. After the discussion, students can role-play each situation.

- Jim notices that his parents are especially pressed for time. He volunteers to help with household chores. This act of giving of his time is an expression of love and concern toward his parents.

- Parents observe that their son William is spending too much time in places or with companions they think may be harmful to him. The parents give their time to put much thought into what is best for the child and to provide more constructive experiences for him.

- A teacher sees that a student is having trouble with an assignment. She shows she cares by giving the student further instruction after school.

- Susan demonstrates respect for education by giving quality time in her classes and assignments. She shows this respect by the ways she uses time in classes as well as with her body language, facial expression, and eye contact with the teacher. Contrast her behavior with that of her friend, Louise, who has poor skills in expressive time usage.

- A teenager is interviewing for a part-time job. The person who has been holding the interview tries to end the meeting by looking at his watch and saying, "Well, thank you very much for coming in. I will be back in touch with you at a later date." The teenager says "You're welcome" and continues to sit there. He has no awareness that the interviewer has signaled that it is time to end the interview. (Note: this is a good opportunity to teach the students how to be aware that someone is signaling that it is time to end a discussion.) Did the person being interviewed receive the message? How should that person have correctly responded?

- Mike is always late and keeps others waiting. He is perceived as being disrespectful and irresponsible by his teachers and friends. In reality, Mike has difficulty judging time and is unaware of the message he is sending by his expression of time. How would you respond to Mike if he asked you why other people don't seem to trust him?

NOTE: Emphasize punctuality to dyssemic students, because judging time is a real problem for many of them. People often have a negative perception of others who are not able to judge time and use it properly. Students need to understand it is important for them to be aware of time, to be on time for class or a job, and to turn assignments in promptly.

CROSS-CHANNELING

Clarification of the Skill

When students have become familiar with the channels of nonverbal communication described in these lessons, they will benefit from exercises that reinforce skills in two or more channels simultaneously. Such activities are called *cross-channeling*.

⇨   Before beginning the cross-channeling exercises, read through them and prepare a list of sentences, paragraphs, and situations, as well as a collection of photographs suitable for illustrating multiple nonverbal language skills. For a list of emotions, see the A to Z of Emotions on pages 180-181.

⇨   Have students practice using the skills of body language and facial expressions through role-playing. Make them aware that their gestures and facial expressions must complement or agree with each other instead of contradicting each other.

NOTE: In order to effectively assist students, choose examples, role-play situations, and discussions that are relevant to the students. It would be less productive to discuss proper ways of standing in line at the bank, for example, than it would be to discuss standing in line at school. Keep discussions and demonstrations centered on topics that directly pertain to students' lives.

Discussion and Activities Using Cross-Channelling

⇨   Present a picture of a person who by facial expression and gesture exhibits anger, and ask the students to use nonverbal language skills to respond in kind. Many situations involving different emotions can be used here.

⇨   Present a paragraph for students to read out loud. As they read, call out an emotion their tone of voice, facial expression, gestures, and postures should express.

⇨   Read a sentence to the students expressing an emotion by tone of voice, then ask the students to use appropriate facial expressions and body language to express the same emotion.

⇨ Describe situations calling for various intensities of smiles or laughter. Reverse the description to include situations in which smiles or laughter would not be appropriate. Ask students to judge the proper intensity for each situation.

⇨ Present the following situations:
  • You have received a gift and are very pleasantly surprised and appreciative. Use voice tone, facial expressions, and gestures to indicate how you feel.
  • A teacher is upset with a student's behavior in class. Demonstrate how the teacher would look and speak and how the student would respond nonverbally.
  • Your friend has just failed a test. How would you comfort that friend nonverbally?
  • Imagine running into someone at a gathering that you usually do not feel comfortable with (a new student or an authority figure). Show how to greet that person in a way which hides your discomfort (with direct eye contact, a smile, and a pleasant voice).

⇨ Show students a picture of a sad face, asking them to give an example of a situation that might cause them to feel this emotion. Ask them to express this situation with a sentence or two, accompanying the verbal description with a sad facial expression. Then ask them to add a gesture and a posture to the facial expression and the sentence. Continue this exercise, using different pictures and different students.

⇨ Play a game called "emotional party."
  1. Have students discuss various emotions, such as:
     • cheerfulness   • surprise   • annoyance
     • contentment   • depression   • fear
  2. Help them define the emotions using the following questions:
     • What situations would cause this emotion?
     • What facial expression would a person exhibit when feeling that emotion?
     • What tone of voice would the person use?
     • What posture would the person use?
     • What gestures would the person use?
  3. Whisper an emotion to the students one by one and ask them to remember it but to keep it a secret. If dealing with a large class, the teacher can ask each student to draw an emotion card from a hat.
  4. Ask the students to think of a situation which might make them feel their

assigned emotion. Have them raise their hands when they have thought of a situation. The teacher can help students by suggesting gestures, etc., that could be used for their specific emotion, as long as other students cannot hear the advice.

5. Select a volunteer to give a party. Arrange the desks in a circle, leaving only the "host" within the circle. Ask the host to pretend to straighten up the "room" for the party while expressing his or her designated emotion.

6. Select a second student to be a "guest." When entering the party, that guest begins immediately to express his or her emotion by relating the situation that caused that emotion. When the host figures out the guest's emotion, the host begins to emulate the guest's actions or emotion by the appropriate use of body language and voice. Only when the guest is certain that the host has accurately picked up on the emotion does the guest take a seat within the circle.

7. Select another "guest." When the new guest enters the circle and begins expressing his or her emotion, this person remains standing until certain that the host and other guest(s) have responded accurately and emulated that particular emotion.

8. This exercise is repeated until all have "attended" the party.

9. Help any students having difficulty receiving or sending accurate messages with their area of difficulty.

When you have completed this course of study with your students, continue to review and practice nonverbal skills in your classroom on a daily basis.

SOME FINAL COMMENTS

Learning nonverbal language is a lifelong endeavor. As new "words" enter this unspoken language we must learn them, and as situations change, we must get used to variations in nonverbal "word" usage. In order to adapt to the ever-changing complexities of social relationships, children and adults must learn to constantly observe and incorporate new nonverbal language.

Once children have learned how to use nonverbal language effectively, their ongoing social success will be dependent not only on what they know, but on an awareness that symbols and signs around us can vary or change. Just as children who are socially successful must know how and when to use appropriate slang and other forms of age-specific speech, so they must attend to the nonverbal patterns that are constantly changing around them. Therefore, any effort to teach nonverbal language must include encouraging an awareness of change throughout life. The children who fail to develop nonverbal language skills often become the adults who suffer interpersonally; children who master these skills can find the lights are always green no matter what road they take.

THE LOTTO BASE BOARD

<table>
<tr><td></td><td></td><td></td></tr>
<tr><td></td><td></td><td></td></tr>
<tr><td></td><td></td><td></td></tr>
</table>

The Lotto Base Board

The lotto base is simply a square board which may be used to assess the child's understanding of a variety of nonverbal behaviors. If you laminate the board, you can write directly on it with nonpermanent markers (instead of using emotion cards).

1. Write down one emotion per square (or place one emotion card in each square).

2. Choose a channel or channels to work on (for example, facial expressions).

3. The sender then tries to convey an emotion through the chosen channel. (If the sender chooses "angry," then he or she makes an angry face.)

4. The receiver tries to interpret nonverbal signals and correctly choose the corresponding emotion on the board.

5. If the receiver chooses the correct emotion, he or she erases the emotion (or turns over the card). If the receiver incorrectly identifies the emotion, the sender moves on to the next emotion.

6. Continue these steps until all emotions have been identified correctly.

Blank Face
The blank face on the following page is for use in facial expressions lessons. Photocopy this image as often as desired, or laminate and reuse.

AN A-Z OF EMOTIONS

Facial Expressions

A Affectionate
Aggravated
Aggressive
Alarmed
Amazed
Amused
Angry
Anguished
Anxious
Apathetic
Apologetic
Argumentative
Arrogant
Ashamed
Assertive
Astonished
Awed

B Bashful
Believing
Bitter
Blue
Boastful
Bored
Brave

C Calm
Cheerful
Concentrating
Concerned
Confident
Confused
Contented
Curious

D Decisive
Defeated
Delighted
Depressed
Desperate
Despondent
Determined
Disappointed

Disapproving
Disbelieving
Discontented
Discouraged
Disgusted
Dismayed
Dissatisfied
Distasteful
Distracted
Distressed
Disturbed
Doubtful

E Eager
Ecstatic
Elated
Embarrassed
Enraged
Enthusiastic
Envious
Exasperated
Exhausted
Exhilarated
Expectant

F Forgetful
Fretful
Frightened
Frustrated
Furious

G Genial
Gleeful
Gloomy
Grateful
Greedy
Grieving
Guilty

H Happy
Helpless
Hesitant
Hopeful

Horrified
Huffy
Humiliated
Humorous
Hurt

I Idiotic
Impressed
Indifferent
Innocent
Insane
Insecure
Inspired
Interested

J Jealous
Joyful

K Kind

L Lazy
Lethargic
Lonely
Lovable

M Manic
Melancholic
Merry
Mischievous
Miserable
Moody
Mopey
Mournful
Mysterious

N Nauseated
Negative
Nervous
Noble

O Obstinate
Optimistic
Overworked

P Panicked
Pained
Passionate
Perplexed
Perturbed
Pitiful
Pleasant
Positive
Pressured
Prim
Proud
Puzzled

Q Queer

R Regretful
Relieved
Remorseful
Resentful
Responsible

S Sad
Satisfied
Sick
Shamed
Shocked
Sorrowful
Stressed
Sulky
Surprised
Suspicious
Sympathetic

T Talkative
Tender
Tense
Timid
Tired
Thoughtful
Threatened
Thrilled
Tortured
Triumphant
Two-faced

V   Vain
    Virtuous
    Vulnerable

W   Warm
    Withdrawn
    Worried

Z   Zealous

Gestures

A   Affectionate
    Aggressive
    Alarmed
    Amazed
    Amused
    Angry
    Anticipatory
    Anxious
    Apathetic
    Apologetic
    Argumentative
    Ashamed
    Assertive
    Astonished

B   Bored
    Brave

C   Calm
    Caring
    Cautious
    Cheerful
    Concentrating
    Confident

D   Defeated
    Delighted
    Disapproving
    Dissatisfied
    Distressed
    Doubtful

E   Eager
    Ecstatic
    Elated
    Embarrassed
    Enraged
    Enthusiastic

    Exasperated
    Exhausted
    Expectant

F   Forgetful
    Frightened
    Frustrated
    Furious

G   Genial
    Gleeful
    Grateful
    Greedy
    Grieving
    Guilty

H   Happy
    Helpful
    Hesitant
    Horrified
    Huffy
    Humiliated
    Hurt

I   Idiotic
    Impressed
    Indifferent
    Insane
    Inspired

J   Joyful

K   Kind

L   Lazy
    Lethargic
    Loving

M   Manic
    Merry
    Mischievous
    Mysterious

N   Nervous
    Noble

O   Obstinate

P   Panicked
    Pained
    Passionate
    Proud

    Pleased

Q   Quiet
    Quick

R   Relieved

S   Sad
    Satisfied
    Shocked
    Stressed
    Sulky
    Surprised
    Sympathetic

T   Tender
    Tense
    Tired
    Thoughtful
    Threatened
    Thrilled
    Triumphant

U   Uncomfortable
    Undecided

V   Virtuous

W   Warm
    Withdrawn
    Worried

Postures

A   Aggravated
    Aggressive
    Agile
    Alarmed
    Angry
    Anticipatory
    Apathetic
    Arrogant
    Ashamed

B   Bashful
    Bored
    Brave

C   Confident
    Contemplative

D   Defeated
    Despondent
    Determined
    Domineering

E   Embarrassed
    Exhausted

F   Frightened
    Furious

G   Guilty

H   Happy

I   Indifferent
    Insecure

L   Lazy

M   Moody
    Mopey
    Mournful

N   Nervous
    Noble

O   Obstinate

R   Regretful
    Remorseful

S   Sad
    Sick
    Shamed
    Shocked
    Sulky
    Surprised
    Suspicious

T   Tense
    Timid
    Tired
    Tortured

V   Vain

W   Withdrawn
    Worried

REFERENCES

Adler, Ronald, and Towne, Neil. *Looking Out/Looking In.* San Francisco: Rinehart Press, 1975.

Bailey, Wendy. "Adult Performance on the Diagnostic Analysis of Nonverbal Accuracy Scale (DANVA): A Survey of African-American and European-American Undergraduate Students." Master's thesis, Emory University, Atlanta, 1995.

Burgoon, Judee, and Saine, Thomas. *The Unspoken Dialogue: An Introduction to Nonverbal Communication.* Boston: Houghton Mifflin, 1978.

Carle, Marlene. "The Effect of Teaching Nonverbal Communication on the Academic Achievement in Written Expression." Master's thesis, Kean College of New Jersey, 1993.

Ekman, Paul, and Friesen, Wallace. "Constants Across Cultures in the Face and Emotion." *Journal of Personality and Social Psychology* 17 (1971): 124–129.

Ekman, Paul, and Friesen, Wallace. *Unmasking the Face.* Englewood Cliffs: Prentice-Hall, 1975.

Hall, Edward. *The Hidden Dimension.* New York: Doubleday, 1966.

Harré, Rom. *Personal Being.* Oxford, England: Blackwell, 1983.

Hickson, Mark, and Stacks, Don. *Nonverbal Communication: Studies and Applications.* Dubuque: Wm. C. Brown, 1967.

Johnson, Doris, and Myklebust, Helmer. *Learning Disabilities: Educational Principles and Practices.* New York: Gruen and Stratton, 1967.

Jourard, Sidney. "An Exploratory Study of Body Accessibility." *British Journal of Social and Clinical Psychology* 5 (1966): 221–231.

Jourard, Sidney, and Rubin, J.E. "Self-disclosure and Touching: A Study of Two Modes of Interpersonal Encounter and their Inter-relation." *Journal of Humanistic Psychology* 8 (1968): 39–48.

Malloy, John. *The New Dress for Success Handbook.* New York: Warner Books, 1988.

Mehrabian, Albert. *Silent Messages.* Belmont: Wadsworth, 1987.

Minskoff, Esther. "Teaching Approach for Developing Nonverbal Communication Skills in Students with Social Perception Deficits: Part I, The Basic Approach and Body Language Cues." *Journal of Learning Disabilities* 13 (1980): 118–124.

Minskoff, Esther. "Teaching Approach for Developing Nonverbal Communication Skills in Students with Social Perception Deficits: Part II, Proxemic, Vocalic, and Artifactual Cues." *Journal of Learning Disabilities* 13 (1980): 203–208.

Morris, Desmond. *Manwatching.* New York: Abrams, 1977.

Nowicki, Stephen, Jr., and Duke, Marshall P. "A Measure of Nonverbal Social Processing Ability in Children Between the Ages of 6 and 10 years of Age." Paper presented at the annual meeting of the American Psychological Society, Alexandria, Virginia, 1989.

Rourke, Byron. "Socioemotional Disturbances of Learning Disabled Children." *Journal of Consulting and Clinical Psychology* 56 (1988): 801–810.

Sapir, Edward. "The Unconscious Patterning of Behavior in Society." In *Selected Writings of Edward Sapir in Language, Culture, and Personality*, edited by E. Mandelbaum. Berkeley: University of California Press, 1949.

Scheff, Thomas. *Being Mentally Ill: A Sociological Theory.* New York: Aldine, 1984.

von Raffler-Engel, Walburga. "Developmental Kinesics." In *Developmental Kinesics: The Emerging Paradigm*, edited by B. Hoffer and R. St. Clair. Baltimore: University Park Press, 1981.

RESOURCES

For information about prepared materials to use in informal and formal assessment and remediation, write to Steve Nowicki and Marshall Duke, Department of Psychology, Emory University, Atlanta, Georgia, 30322. While not exhaustive, the list of books, publishers, agencies, and organizations below can provide guidance to those seeking help in understanding and working with dyssemic children.

Books and Periodicals

Casey, L. *Children, Problems, and Guidelines: A Resource Book for Schools and Parents*. East Aurora, NY: Slosson Educational Publications.

Cordoni, B. *Living with a Learning Disability* (revised edition). Carbondale: Southern Illinois University Press. P.O. Box 3697, Carbondale, IL 62902-3697.

Dias, P. *Diamonds in the Rough*. East Aurora, NY: Slosson Educational Publications.

Directory of Facilities and Services for the Learning Disabled. Published biannually by Academic Therapy Publications. 20 Commercial Blvd., Novato, CA 94949-6191. (415) 883-3314.

The Directory for Exceptional Children. Published biannually by Porter Sargent Publishers, Inc. 11 Beacon Street, Boston, MA 02108. (617) 523-1670.

Dowrick, P.W. *Social Survival for Children*. New York: Brunner/Mazel, 1986.

LDA News Brief (published bimonthly); *Multidisciplinary Journal* (published biannually). Learning Disabilities Association. 4156 Library Road, Pittsburgh, PA 15234. (412) 341-1515.

Osman, Betty B. *No One to Play With: The Social Side of Learning Disabilities*. New York: Random House, 1982.

Publishers

Academic Therapy Publications. 20 Commercial Blvd., Novato, CA 94949-6191. (415) 883-3314.

Ann Arbor Publishers. P.O. Box 7249, Naples, FL 33940. (813) 775-3528.

Association for Childhood International. 11501 Georgia Avenue, Suite 315, Wheaton, MD 20902. (301) 942-2443.

Learning Disabilities Association. 4156 Library Road, Pittsburgh, PA 15234. (412) 341-1515.

Clinical Psychology Publishing Co. 4 Conant Square, Brandon, VT 05733. (802) 247-6871.

Porter Sargent Publishers. 11 Beacon Street, Boston, MA 02108. (617) 523-1670.

Slosson Educational Publications, Inc. P.O. Box 280, East Aurora, NY 14052. (716) 652-0930.

Agencies and Organizations

American Psychological Association. 750 First Street N.E., Washington, D.C. 20002-4242. (202) 336-5500. (Also local and state psychological associations.)

American Psychiatric Association. 1400 K Street N.W., Washington, D.C. 20005. (202) 682-6000. (Also local and state medical or psychiatric societies.)

Council for Exceptional Children. 1920 Association Dr., Reston, VA 22091. (703) 620-3660.

National Learning Disabilities Association (LDA) of America. 4156 Library Road, Pittsburgh, PA 15234. Information and Referral: (412) 341-1515. Free material about learning disabilities. The National LDA can put you in touch with the chapter nearest you; there are 500 chapters across the country.

National Information Center for Children and Youth with Disabilities. P.O. Box 1492, Washington, D.C. 20013-1492. (800) 695-0285

U.S. Department of Education—Office of Special Education. 600 Independence Avenue S.W., Washington, D.C. 20202. (202) 205-5507.

MARSHALL P. DUKE received his Ph.D. in clinical psychology from Indiana University. Charles Howard Candler Professor of Personality and Psychopathology, he chairs Emory University's department of psychology. He has published over fifty scholarly articles and co-authored (with Stephen Nowicki, Jr.) *Helping the Child Who Doesn't Fit In* as well as a textbook of abnormal psychology.

STEPHEN NOWICKI, JR. received his Ph.D. from Purdue University. He is the author of over 150 publications and presentations and the coauthor (with Marshall Duke) of *Helping the Child Who Doesn't Fit In* and an abnormal psychology textbook. Dr. Nowicki has received two Fulbright awards and serves as Charles Howard Candler Professor of Psychology at Emory University.

ELISABETH A. MARTIN received her B.S. and Bachelor of Education degrees from the University of Newcastle upon Tyne, England, and her M.Ed. with specialization in Special Education (Dyslexia) from the University of Kingston upon Thames, England. Ms. Martin has taught learning disabled students at the Dyslexia Institute in England and at several specialty schools in the United States.